TRAINING TEACHERS OF THE
GIFTED AND TALENTED

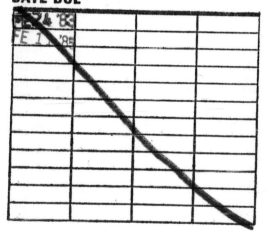

Perspectives on Gifted and Talented Education

Elementary and Secondary Level Programs for the Gifted
   and Talented
Gifted Young Children
Identification of the Gifted
Reaching Out: Advocacy for the Gifted and Talented
Somewhere to Turn: Strategies for Parents of Gifted and
   Talented Children
Training Teachers of the Gifted and Talented

TRAINING TEACHERS OF THE GIFTED AND TALENTED

Margaret Lindsey

Professor Emeritus
Teachers College, Columbia University

Perspectives on Gifted and Talented Education

Abraham J. Tannenbaum
Director

Elizabeth Neuman
Editor

Gifted and Talented Project
Teachers College, Columbia University

Teachers College, Columbia University
New York and London   1980

This work was developed under a contract with the U.S. Office of
Education, Department of Health, Education, and Welfare. However, the
content does not necessarily reflect the position or policy of that Agency,
and no official endorsement of these materials should be inferred.

Library of Congress Cataloging in Publication Data
Lindsey, Margaret.
    Training teachers of the gifted and talented.

    (Perspectives on gifted and talented education)
    Bibliography: p.
    Includes index.
    1.   Teachers of gifted children—Training of.
I. Title. II. Series.
LC3993.25.L56   371.95   80-11867
ISBN 0-8077-2590-0

Design by Romeo Enriquez
        8   7   6   5   4   3   2   1
80   81   82   83   84   85   86   87
Printed in the U.S.A.

CONTENTS

TABLES

FIGURES

FOREWORD

GIFTED CHILDREN WHO draw attention to themselves—and not all do—through their precocity are constantly in the public eye, sometimes as stars, sometimes as sties. They cannot be ignored, but they can be neglected. Professionals and laymen alike have often reacted ambivalently to these children, appreciating their special qualities while doubting their right to special educational enrichment on the grounds that it smacks of elitism. There are educators who believe that the gifted can make it on their own without extra help and regard differentiated programs for such children as luxuries that are welcome when they are affordable and quickly disposable when they are not. What counts most according to this point of view is the "golden mean," or normalcy, as reflected in the normal curve of ability and performance. Whoever fails to measure up to the golden mean has a right to every kind of compensatory assistance; whoever exceeds levels of functioning that are normal or average for most children may receive applause but no extra attention. Rarely is thought given to the possibility that democratic education means stretching each child's mind to its own outer limits without injury to mental or physical health.

Fortunately growing interest in the gifted at school is helping sharpen public concern for the individualities of *all* children. Differentiated education is beginning to replace procrustean education, and fewer people are making a fetish of averageness in the normal curve. Yet, this new awareness that "sameness" and "equality" are *not* synonymous terms when they refer to educational opportunity has not always led to a clear understanding of existing knowledge in the field. A great many myths have masqueraded as truisms, and they tend to be reinforced rather than exploded in some of the awareness rallies, lectures, and workshops on behalf of gifted children. Even the professional literature has been affected by unsubstantiated claims about the nature and nurture of giftedness and by rhetoric that appeals more to the emotions than to reason.

It is time that some clearer impressions were recorded about the "state of the art" in understanding and educating the gifted in order to counterbalance some of the distortions, wishful thinking, overblown claims, and misdirected evangelism that has plagued the field. The intention of this Teachers College series of original monographs is to contribute to that kind of corrective. It has grown out of a federally supported contract to develop information products on key topics pertaining to the gifted and to bring them to the attention of the general public, including laymen and professionals. The authors have devoted considerable care to the content of their statements and the consequent impact on readers. Each writer is eminently qualified to make a balanced, meaningful contribution that avoids simply paraphrasing what others have said earlier. The aim is to inform through cogent presentations that can be appreciated by the widest possible audience ranging from those who want to be initiated to those who seek new insights into the field of educating the gifted.

Abraham J. Tannenbaum
Teachers College, Columbia University

PREFACE

Although this book focuses on the education of teachers who will work with gifted youngsters and is addressed primarily to those responsible for teaching teachers, whether in colleges and universities, schools, teacher centers, or elsewhere, it is concerned with the development of all children's potential, whether gifted or not, and all teachers' education, whether specialized or not. The current emphasis on mainstreaming means that most gifted children will remain in regular classrooms most of the time. Yet what has been found to help regular teachers fulfill their responsibility to the gifted will benefit all children. Thus the book is written as much with parents, school board members, and legislators in mind as teachers, school administrators, and teacher educators.

The approach rests on the premise that the same principles advocated for guiding the development of the gifted should guide the education of teachers too. The emphasis is on what is lacking, what changes need to be made, and what processes or theories of designing educational programs are most effective in producing the desired changes.

M.L.

1

CURRENT TRENDS IN THE EDUCATION OF TEACHERS FOR THE GIFTED

Interest in the educational needs of the gifted and talented in American schools has waxed and waned since public schooling first began. In the late fifties and early sixties, for example, the brief attention given to a discipline-centered curriculum was accompanied by a spurt of renewed interest in the education of the gifted, or at least academically gifted.* But for the rest of the decade the emphasis swung toward developing the competencies of all students, through mainstreaming coupled with individualized instruction. However, in 1971, when a national survey by the U.S. Commissioner of Education (Marland) revealed how few educational programs there were for the gifted, indeed, how few of the gifted had even been identified, interest in their education was sparked anew. Out of an estimated two million or more gifted children in the public schools, only four percent appeared to be receiving an appropriate education. Most of the administrators surveyed seemed unconcerned. More than half said they had no gifted and talented children in their schools. Only 12 institutions of higher education were found to be providing graduate level programs for teachers specializing in education for the gifted (Marland, 1972).

Today the picture is markedly changed. Since 1972, when an Office of Gifted and Talented Education was established within the U.S. Office of Education and federal funds began to flow to projects concerning the gifted, more courses and graduate programs for teachers specializing in their education have emerged, and more in-service programs and workshops to help classroom teachers identify the gifted and meet their needs have been set up. New ways to group gifted pupils together have been tried, often in combination with mainstreaming, such as regular class participation along with special classes. New ways to accommodate the gifted without special grouping have also been explored. Various models for their acceleration have been developed.

---

*For example, The Talented Youth Project of the Horace Mann-Lincoln Institute of School Experimentation, Teachers College, Columbia University. See also M. Gold, *Education of the intellectually gifted*. Columbus, OH: Merrill, 1965.

A body of knowledge is accumulating not only about the characteristics of the gifted and the kinds of learning and social experiences they need, but also about the characteristics of the teachers who are most successful with them, the competencies they need to possess, and the kinds of behavior as persons and as professionals they need to demonstrate. Since the success of any program rests ultimately on the teachers, the most influential factor in a student's life, it is encouraging that more money is going toward their education, that more courses and more graduate programs are being offered in the field, and that more states are setting standards to certify teachers for the gifted. But on closer look, there still remains much to be desired.

FEDERAL FUNDING

In fiscal 1979 the Office of Gifted and Talented Education in the Department of Education reported that it had disbursed approximately three million dollars (Bokee, 1979). These monies funded six leadership training programs and four model projects as well as programs sponsored by 38 local education agencies and 37 state educational agencies.

Of course, this is not the whole story. Funds are allocated to the education of the gifted, directly or indirectly, by other federal agencies, by state and local agencies, and by philanthropic institutions. The real total is difficult to estimate, but the current concern about meeting the educational needs of the gifted is clear. The activity underway is wide in scope, encompassing direct service to all age groups in all types of giftedness—pre- and in-service education of personnel, planning, implementing, and evaluating programs, and first steps in much needed research on personnel development.

STATE CERTIFICATION

In late 1978, a survey (Benjamin) was conducted to find out what, if anything, state departments of education were doing about certifying teachers to work with gifted and talented persons. Of the 41 responses received, only ten states reported that they had already adopted special requirements governing their certification and that they went beyond those for teaching in regular classrooms or in special education generally. Eighteen states indicated that requirements were under consideration. One indicated that no special requirements were to be set. The idea had not yet been considered in 12 states but likely would be in the near future.

Usually certification requires that a candidate already has a regular teaching certificate, has taught successfully at least one year, and has taken from nine to 18 semester hours of graduate study, including a practicum, in the field.

But there are exceptions. For example, North Carolina offers a competency-based evaluation as an alternative to course work.

Teachers applying for certification through the Competency-Based Program will be evaluated on the basis of knowledge of information and principles about the gifted and talented program and demonstrated competency in applying this. . . .
   The major emphasis . . . however, will be centered around the teacher's ability to develop and implement effectively a comprehensive instructional plan. (North Carolina State Department of Public Instruction, 1976, pp. 1, 3)

COLLEGE AND UNIVERSITY PROGRAMS

   In 1977 a partial study (Bruch et al.) was made, through state contacts, of what colleges and universities in the southern states are doing with respect to special programs for teachers of the gifted and talented. Results of the survey are summarized in Table 1.

Table 1: Type and Frequency of Programs in Colleges and Universities for Teachers of the Gifted and Talented

Program Classification	Number of Programs Reported
No information received or no courses, degree, or certification programs indicated	10
Courses, but no degree or certification programs	36
Summer only	7
Certification programs	14
Undergraduate degree program, with major	1
Undergraduate degree program, with minor	3
Graduate master's degree, with major	27
Graduate master's degree, with minor	20
Specialist's degree, with major	4
Specialist's degree, with minor	3
Doctoral degree, with major	9
Doctoral degree, with minor	7
Graduate degree programs planned, not in effect	12

   The survey is consistent with reports from other state education agencies in at least three respects: (1) many courses are offered that do not lead to degrees in education of the gifted; (2) almost all the more specialized study in the education of the gifted is at the graduate level; and (3) admission to graduate programs requires a candidate to have a teaching certificate and at least one year's teaching experience. In addition, most programs fall either in special education or psychology departments, and course titles tend to be overbroad and generalized.

Even more discouraging, few courses seem to be specifically designed to help regular classroom teachers identify or meet the needs of the gifted students in their classes. Instead regular teachers who take such courses are expected to move into new roles, teaching in special arrangements for the gifted, although most of the gifted will spend most of their time in regular classrooms. A brief look at programs in two states, both of which have adopted certification regulations for teachers of the gifted, will illustrate.

In North Carolina (1976) the courses in one program approved by the state for both certification and a master's degree in education of the gifted, are listed in Table 2.

**Table 2: Certification and Master's Degree in
Education of the Gifted, North Carolina**

Title (Semester Hours)	*Content*
1. Orientation to Human Exceptionality (3)	Overview of various types of exceptional children and adults. Emphasis on characteristics, identification, educational programming, and management.
2. Diagnostic-Prescriptive Teaching (3)	Specific teaching techniques of subjects for the exceptional child, arithmetic, reading, art, music, physical activities and recreation, and social studies.
3. Psychological and Sociological Problems of Exceptional Children (3)	Cultural, social, and intellectual factors, therapeutic problems, and issues in special education.
4. Counseling Parents of Exceptional Children (3)	Techniques and considerations.
5. Interpretation of Assessment Data (3)	The administration, scoring, and diagnostic interpretation of tests commonly used.
6. Research and Bibliography (2)	A study of procedures, designs, and methods of reporting in human resources.

7. Advanced Curriculum Design (3)

The physiological and psychological basis of learning, and curriculum development for various exceptionalities.

8. Curriculum for the Gifted/Talented (3)

An introductory course in curriculum development.

9. Nature and Nurture of Gifted and Talented (3)

A survey of educational programs for the gifted, including curriculum and administrative adjustments.

10. Creativity (3)

Techniques to enhance creativity in teachers and students.

11. Selected Topic: Higher Cognitive Processes (3)

Various classifications and approaches with application in the classroom.

12. Seminar in Reading (3)

The reading needs of specific gifted groups.

13. Internship: Gifted (1–8)

Intensive internship teaching gifted children.

As can be seen, the program requires 35 semester hours of course work plus an internship, for which a student may receive from one to eight semester hours of credit. Of the 13 courses required, one (number 8) appears to be appropriate for all teachers and other educators (an introductory course in curriculum); the first seven seem to be courses in exceptionality for students in any area of special education; the last five appear to be designed specifically for teachers intending to work with gifted and talented students.

At the University of Georgia, the Department of Educational Psychology (1977) offers a multileveled graduate program in the area of education for the gifted ranging from the minimum course work required for supplementary certification through certification and a master's degree to a doctoral program. The courses centered on the gifted are:

> Characteristics of the Gifted
> Tests and Measurements
> Assessment of Gifted Children and Youth
> Strategies and Materials for the Gifted
> Learning Difficulties of Gifted Children and Youth.

Along with a practicum and internship, there is development and field testing in five areas:

Curricular materials

Workshops

In-service packages

Administrative, i.e., plans for program development, administrative schemes for school districts

Applied or theoretical research.

Again, the more specialized study is only at the graduate level, and admission requires that a candidate has had a year's teaching experience. It might be said that such graduate programs fall into the category of in-service education, but they are mainly for teachers seeking advanced degrees and planning to leave the regular classroom. Still teachers who intend to go on teaching in regular classrooms and want to learn more about the gifted and their development may, if time, money, and scheduling permit, pursue one or more of the many courses offered.

WORKSHOPS AND SEMINARS

There are variations on college and university courses. One, called "Teach-in: Challenging Gifted/Talented K–12—A Cross-Curricular Approach" (Grant, 1978), was a summer weekend series of graduate-level sessions at William Paterson College in New Jersey that led to four credits. Participants were notified in advance that they would be required to "submit a practical or publishable product for use with gifted/talented on or before the final session." Each weekend was devoted to one or more of a wide range of topics, also announced in advance, such as:

Provoking expression

Science techniques for the gifted

Reading for the gifted

Independent art/craft enrichment activities

Social science for the gifted

Using media with the gifted

Gifts for the gifted: Language arts and social sciences

Freeing gifted to write through reading

Mind games: explorations in intellectual creativity.

Many agencies besides colleges and universities, of course, are conducting workshops or seminars. For example, the Las Vegas school system held a laboratory seminar for teachers of the gifted called "You Through The Ages." The National/State Leadership Training Institute for the Gifted and Talented conducted a month-long summer project in Los Angeles that brought 62 students and 32 teachers together to "educate one another" (Curry & Sato, 1977). The combination of classwork and involvement with the students, along with lectures and work sessions by nationally recognized experts in the field, gave the program unique value. The principles of training that guided the workshop, opening it to a wide range of teachers and school personnel, are worth noting: training was designed to meet various levels of expertise, to serve individuals with different roles, to meet the specific needs of participants, to be problem- and product-oriented, and to be team-centered.

The short-term workshop is a compromise, but as J.S. Renzulli (1977) has pointed out, a valuable one:

The one-shot "dog-and-pony show" type of workshop conducted by a charismatic visiting "expert" might provide us with the inspiration needed to get started, but a more organized approach is required if there is going to be any follow-through and long-term benefits.

In the area of the gifted and talented, we are faced with somewhat of a dilemma. On the one hand, there is an almost urgent need to prepare qualified teachers for the rapidly growing number of school programs that serve this segment of the student population. At the same time, there are a limited number of undergraduate and graduate training programs, many teachers are unable to participate in full-time study, and limited human and financial resources prohibit the implementation of comprehensive (long-term) training programs. Thus, the short-term workshop represents one of the few viable alternatives for meeting training needs in this area of special education. (pp. 186 –187)

CONCLUSION

The money made available for teacher education and leadership training, as well as for research, experimentation, and materials production, may contribute substantially to theoretical knowledge and practice concerning the education of the gifted. Standards for special certification of personnel in the field may increase the number and adequacy of persons prepared to assume various roles in planning and conducting educational programs for the gifted. Specialized offerings in colleges and universities and in-service workshops and seminars may provide inspiration, augment knowledge and skills, and accelerate the willingness of classroom teachers and other professionals to make provisions for the gifted.

Knowledge is mounting rapidly; at least more is known about a few things in connection with the education of the gifted, although some important questions, while recognized, have not yet been addressed. These developments are important, but the sum of them all can be only as effective as the teacher makes them in daily contact with the gifted, whether in a regular classroom or in special classes.

The current commitment to individualized instruction and mainstreaming requires a new look at the whole of education, not only teachers and their teaching strategies, but also learning environments, curricular designs, administrative practices, class standards, and expectancies. But first, and most important, there is need to go beyond mechanical arrangements and practices so common at present in individualized instruction. Despite all the advances, many gifted children are still not identified; many talents of "average" students are still not recognized.

2

THE KINDS OF
TEACHERS
NEEDED

U<small>NLESS GIFTED</small> persons are identified early and provisions made for the development of their great potential, it is likely that they will succumb all too readily to what is for them ritual, routine, and low expectancies in a school setting, develop feelings of boredom, and fail to recognize and use the special talents they possess.

Since most of the gifted will probably spend most of their time in a regular classroom, it is essential that all teachers, and especially classroom teachers, have both the commitment and the capacity to identify the gifted and meet their needs. While special programs exist at the graduate level for special teachers of the gifted —those who work in special arrangements outside the regular classrooms or with the exceptionally gifted—pre-service and in-service programs must provide specific help to enable all teachers to identify and develop talents of the gifted as part of their responsibility to develop the potential of all students. As it is, however, not only are many of the gifted in today's schools overlooked, but many types of giftedness are largely ignored by both the schools and teacher training programs. If the concept of mainstreaming is to be successfully implemented, several conditions will have to be created.

First of all, regular classroom teachers need to be sensitized to the characteristics of the gifted, to develop the simple observation and diagnostic skills required in the initial identification of the gifted, and to build a repertoire of strategies for making special provisions for them in regular classrooms. They need also to be informed about resources beyond the regular classroom and about referral procedures for making contact between a gifted student and an appropriate resource.

All this means that programs to prepare regular classroom teachers should be re-examined to see if they actually do ready prospective teachers, and perhaps more urgently practicing teachers, to meet the demands placed upon them by mainstreaming. Such a re-examination requires the joint efforts of generalists and specialists in teacher education.

ABILITY TO IDENTIFY THE GIFTED

How are the gifted identified? At present information is available on the characteristics of academically and verbally gifted children; less is known about "creative" children; and far less about children with special leadership abilities or talents in the performing and visual arts. Thus many lists of identifying characteristics, while admitting their narrow scope, give rise to stereotypes. For example, one list (Nelson & Cleland, 1975), while noting, "there is no entirely adequate composite of traits for the gifted child," gave "several compilations which provide a basis for the teacher in the identification of gifted children." Included are the following items that apply primarily to the verbally gifted:

> Longer attention span
> Larger vocabulary
> Greater fluency of ideas
> Greater intellectual curiosity
> More rapid and efficient learning
> Greater ability to generalize and form concepts
> Greater insight into problems
> More curiosity and interest in intellectual tasks
> Earlier reading attainment (sometimes before school entrance)
> Wider range of interests.

Teachers should be aware also of certain traits and behaviors that characterize highly creative children:

> Less concern with convention and authority
> More independence in judgment and thinking
> Keener sense of humor
> Less concern with order and organization
> A more temperamental nature.

In addition to lists of narrow scope, some of the usually given characteristics of the gifted have been outdated by further research, and some lists are so generalized that they downplay outstanding but one-dimensional giftedness in a specific aptitude, skill, or behavior. The work at Johns Hopkins University with junior high youths who are precocious in mathematics, and more recently in language (Maeroff, 1979; Stanley, Keating & Fox, 1979), is one among other encouraging examples of moving from generality to specificity in investigating giftedness.

What is particularly unfortunate is that, while the usual school program provides a gifted child the opportunity to exercise his or her academic or verbal gifts, at least to some degree, there is little opportunity to express other kinds of talents. Indeed, it is still true that schools and colleges cater much more to intellectually gifted individuals than to those with other kinds of gifts, in spite of the fact that "gifted and talented" has been defined, by Public Law 93-380, as possession of "demonstrated or potential abilities that give evidence of high performance capability in areas such as *intellectual, creative, academic, or leadership ability or in the performing and visual arts*" (italics added).

Few federally funded projects focus on the identification or development of those talented in the performing arts. No effort to identify or develop those with outstanding leadership capabilities is discernible, yet if schools are to be able to foster the development of all kinds of gifts, in all kinds of children, we need to know much much more about those categories of giftedness that have thus far received so little attention. The considerable research already done on the characteristics of unusually creative adults, in the arts or in leadership roles, could provide an initial basis for investigation.

PERSONAL AND PROFESSIONAL CHARACTERISTICS REQUIRED

Contemporary literature is replete with systematic studies of the kinds of experiences all students need and the kinds of teacher behaviors that best promote their optimal development. It is, of course, the definition of the kinds of experiences gifted children need that by and large determines the characteristics or behaviors required of their teachers.

Taxonomies of the learning process, for example, have been used extensively in suggesting types of experiences students ought to have and the teacher behaviors that facilitate them. The Bloom (1956) taxonomy of cognitive development, which was designed to help teachers stimulate students beyond the less demanding processes of simple recall, comprehension, and application toward the more demanding processes of analysis, synthesis, and evaluation, appears to be the most popular.

F.E. Williams (1971) has presented a broad model that relates three basic components of both affective and cognitive development: the curriculum (subject matter content), teacher behaviors, and pupil behaviors. As can be seen in Figure 1, 18 different teacher behaviors or strategies are identified.

J.P. Guilford's work (1967) on the structure of the intellect and his forceful expositions on the nature and significance of divergent thinking, where the emphasis on the one "right" answer gives way to a number of possible solutions, has underscored its importance for the gifted.

The pioneer study of thinking in elementary school children by H. Taba and her associates (1964) has stimulated considerable attention to the higher cognitive processes and to ways teachers, through their behavior, may "lift" the level of cognition in which children are engaged. Their conclusion that asking questions is probably the single most important thing a teacher does to stimulate higher cognitive processes in children is responsible to a great extent for the wide attention given to research and training on questioning strategies in recent years.

Figure 1: A Model for Implementing Cognitive-Affective Behaviors in the Classroom,

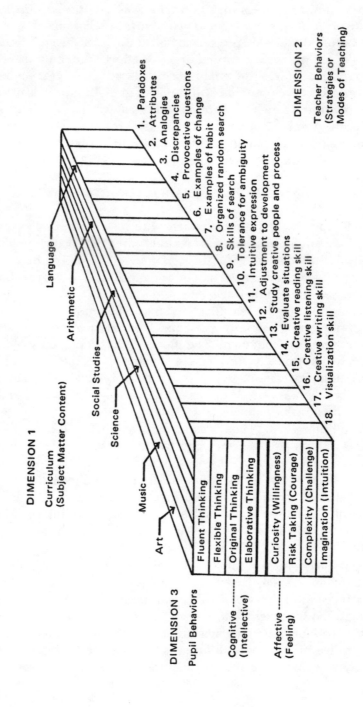

D1 ⇄ D2 ⟶ D3

DIMENSION 1

Curriculum
(Subject Matter Content)

Language

Arithmetic

Social Studies

Science

Music

Art

DIMENSION 3
Pupil Behaviors

Cognitive - - - - - - -
(Intellective)

Affective - - - - - - -
(Feeling)

Fluent Thinking
Flexible Thinking
Original Thinking
Elaborative Thinking

Curiosity (Willingness)
Risk Taking (Courage)
Complexity (Challenge)
Imagination (Intuition)

1. Paradoxes
2. Attributes
3. Analogies
4. Discrepancies
5. Provocative questions
6. Examples of change
7. Examples of habit
8. Organized random search
9. Skills of search
10. Tolerance for ambiguity
11. Intuitive expression
12. Adjustment to development
13. Study creative people and process
14. Evaluate situations
15. Creative reading skill
16. Creative listening skill
17. Creative writing skill
18. Visualization skill

DIMENSION 2

Teacher Behaviors
(Strategies or
Modes of Teaching)

Source: From "Models for Encouraging Creativity in the Classroom" by F.E. Williams, *Educa-*
tional Technology **magazine, 1969,** *ix* **(12), 12. Copyright 1969 by Educational Technology Publications, Inc. Reprinted by permission.**

Such taxonomies help to define stimulating and rewarding kinds of experiences for students and their implications for teacher behaviors. They represent only one approach, however, to defining preferred learning experiences for children and essential behaviors of teachers. Numerous other specialists have, by systematic observation and experimental research, provided analyses of productive teacher behaviors. Not surprisingly, the characteristics found to be desired in regular teachers were even more desired in teachers of the gifted. As one surveyor, Milton J. Gold (1965), noted, "Since the good teacher in general must be a paragon of pedagogic virtues, the teacher prescribed for the gifted by various authorities, pupils, and parents, turns out to be a paragon of paragons" (pp. 412–413). Gold has compiled the characteristics listed in a dozen important works published in the decade of the fifties. Ten years later, a second survey (Maker, 1975) of the qualities found to be essential for teachers of the gifted showed many of the same items listed earlier but backed by more substantial investigation and specificity, though again limited, until quite recently, to concern for the academically or verbally gifted.

A synthesis of what is known about the personal characteristics and teaching behaviors needed by those working with the gifted can be outlined as follows:

Personal Characteristics

> Understands, accepts, respects, trusts, and likes self; has outstanding ego strength
> Is sensitive to others, less concerned with self; supports, respects, trusts others
> Is above average intellectually; exhibits an intellectual style of conceptualizing, generalizing, creating, initiating, relating, organizing, imagining
> Is flexible, open to new ideas
> Has intellectual interests, literary and cultural
> Desires to learn, increase knowledge; has high achievement needs
> Is enthusiastic
> Is intuitive, perceptive
> Is committed to excellence
> Feels reponsible for own behavior and consequences

Personal-Professional Predispositions

> To guide rather than to coerce or pressure
> To be democratic rather than autocratic
> To focus on process as well as product
> To be innovative and experimental rather than conforming

To use problem-solving procedures rather than jump to unfounded conclusions

To seek involvement of others in discovery rather than give out answers

Teaching Behaviors

Develops a flexible, individualized program

Creates a warm, safe, and permissive atmosphere

Provides feedback

Uses varied strategies

Respects personal self-images and enhances positive ones; respects personal values

Respects creativity and imagination

Stimulates higher-order mental processes

Respects individuality and personal integrity.

The range of characteristics may be viewed in three layers. A successful teacher of the gifted is first of all an excellent regular teacher. In addition to that, she or he must possess those characteristics known to be important in working with any gifted student. Finally, the teacher needs the specific competencies related to the specific type of giftedness—intellectual, creative, leadership, or artistic (see Figure 2). Do such "paragons of paragons" exist? Or can such characteristics be developed? For the most part, happily, the answer is yes.

Figure 2: Layers of Qualifications for Teaching the Gifted and Talented

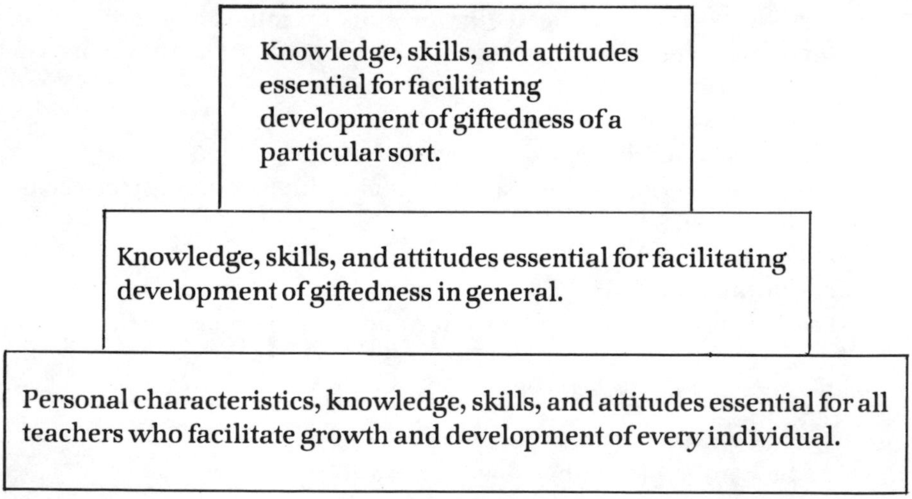

Knowledge, skills, and attitudes essential for facilitating development of giftedness of a particular sort.

Knowledge, skills, and attitudes essential for facilitating development of giftedness in general.

Personal characteristics, knowledge, skills, and attitudes essential for all teachers who facilitate growth and development of every individual.

3

DEVELOPING TALENTED TEACHERS

TEACHERS may be helped to develop the personal and professional characteristics needed to work with the gifted in three ways by assisting them to acquire self-understanding and sensitivity to others, a knowledge of learning and development, and the skills needed to teach effectively. Most programs for teachers do provide theoretical background and teaching skills, but the focus here is on the often neglected areas of strategic importance.

DEVELOPING SELF-UNDERSTANDING AND SENSITIVITY TO OTHERS

Unless a teacher understands, respects, trusts, likes himself or herself, and is similarly sensitive to and supporting of others, no amount of professional knowledge or skill is likely to be of effective help in educating the gifted. Time and again, the literature in the field states that a teacher of the gifted must have outstanding ego strength and must be a person who responds productively to challenge, can take criticism well, and does not suffer stress when working with persons more able and more knowledgeable than he or she is. Such a person, it is said, must have an unusually healthy self-concept. Can this be developed? Much is known today about the ways in which self-concept can be changed.

Combs and his associates (1971) speak of self-concept as not only the product but the "producer of experience."

For each person, his self-concept is who he is. It is the center of his universe . . . and the vantage point from which all else is observed and comprehended. . . . Its very existence determines what else he may perceive. . . . /it/ provides a screen through which everything else is seen, heard, evaluated, understood (p. 41–42).

One is not born with a self-concept. It is developed over time by experience; it is learned. Consciously or unconsciously one observes one's own behavior and its consequences and draws conclusions about the self as able or unable to cope, successful or failing, attractive or unattractive, and informed or uninformed. Such conclusions are also drawn from a person's perceptions of how others view him or her.

One's view of self changes slowly; a person will go to great lengths to maintain an established view even in face of evidence to the contrary. But self-concepts do change, and persons who overestimate or underestimate themselves can be helped to gain a more realistic view of themselves. The change depends on self-correction, and a student in the process of developing must be helped to feel successful.

Students (whether undergraduates or practicing teachers) can be helped in at least three mutually reinforcing ways to understand and, if necessary, change their self-concepts. First, since self-concept is the result of experience, it is possible to design opportunities for experiences that invite constructive self-examination. Second, since the self-view is composed of perceptions of how others feel about one, such perceptions can be brought into the open and their validity examined. Finally, self-concept can be modified by increasing a student's skills or knowledge.

In such a sensitive area, indirect approaches, especially in the initial stages, are best. First a general study of the psychology of self-understanding is advised so that students may come to know that they are dealing with a common phenomenon before they try to help themselves, or their students, in self-understanding. By gaining skill in discussing feelings generally, students are better prepared later to discuss their own feelings or self-view with others. The skills of listening, of trying to understand expressions of feelings without placing a value judgment on them, and of interviewing are all useful in helping oneself and others in self-examination and in becoming sensitive to the needs and perceptions of others.

Following a general preparation, student teachers can collect or devise various instruments and techniques designed to help youngsters express their feelings or values. These may range from various types of inventories to unfinished sentences or paragraphs, autobiographies, or projective techniques making use of pictures. Student teachers can criticize such materials, discuss their possible uses with youngsters, and even try out some of them with children.

The next step is for student teachers to examine their own self-views, privately and on a voluntary basis. Various instruments for this can be used or adapted.* For example, titles like "Important Years of My Life," "What Do I Value?" "Experiences That Make Me Sad, Happy," "Strength Acknowledgments," and "Whom Do I Admire (or Envy) and Why?" have been suggested.

Students could also keep a diary in which they record questions or comments about their own behavior by pupils, peers, college instructors, and others that might have implications for self-correction and note anecdotes about their own behavior that may reveal patterns, such as a tendency to think in stereo-

---

*For a description of pertinent instruments, techniques, and use by one individual in self-study, see Thompson, F.K. *Humane defined: A definition of self as humane teacher*, unpublished doctoral dissertation, Teachers College, Columbia University, New York, 1978. It includes a helpful bibliography on self-study.

types or to become unnecessarily irritated. Keeping the results of such self-study private, but discussing the techniques used with others could lead to a voluntary exchange of self-assessments among students, in self-selected pairs or small groups where students feel secure enough to reveal private thoughts and assessments.

Possibly, where trust of self and others is strong and secure, "rap" sessions in a larger group might be tried, but this device should be used with extreme caution. It should never be a required, or even a socially pressured, activity and should never be conducted by amateurs or professionals who are inexperienced in the method, in the ways to spot danger signals, or in the ways to prevent a person from being destroyed.

Student teachers who join together in the search for more self-understanding have probably taken long strides in increasing their sensitivity to others. They have come to empathize with each person's need to preserve his or her own wholeness. They have had experience at looking at two or more sides to a question. They have seen how important it is that there be room for people to be different. When such first-hand experiences are linked vicariously to others through literature, film, photography, dance, mime, and drama, students gain a store of meanings to take into encounters with various kinds of gifted individuals. Such a storehouse is especially important for students who will teach the exceptionally gifted. So too is a developed sensitivity to the effect of a life history on a person, for the highly gifted, even more than the gifted, are likely to bear certain scars from episodes in life where they have been misunderstood, underestimated, or perhaps envied or disliked because of their own shortcomings in handling their giftedness.

If nothing else, students should come to understand the phenomenon of "winning" in its broader sense. A teacher of the gifted does not have to win every point with a student to earn respect. A difference of opinion can be allowed to go unresolved until more facts are secured. There is often more than one right answer or no right answer at all. Questions or hypothetical statements can replace dogmatic pronouncements. Other experts besides the teacher can be consulted. A teacher can admit being wrong if that is the case. In such ways teachers, by example, help students learn to be less dogmatic and more understanding of the desirability of having as many winners as possible. This fosters healthy self-concepts along with respect for others.

THE BASE OF KNOWLEDGE REQUIRED

Without recourse to a knowledge base upon which to plan their strategies, teachers succumb to thoughtless habit or imitation, and their performance does not rise above a craft. That teachers perform as professionals is essential to all education; for those who work with the gifted it is crucial. The kind of knowledge base they need has four areas: (1) a knowledge of self and sensitivity to others, already discussed, (2) knowledge of human development and the processes of learning, (3) knowledge of the content to be taught, and (4) knowledge about teaching processes.

In each of these last three areas the aim should be to foster the spirit of continual learning. Thus a student should be expected to acquire, beyond information, depth in understanding:

The central questions or principles around which information is or can be organized
The methods by which information is discovered and verified
The social and ethical implications of the information and its use
The relevance of the information to the practice of teaching.

Emphasis on this four-pronged approach in each of the four areas will make explicit the pedagogical principles or assumptions about how a novice acquires knowledge, how a teacher facilitates that process, and how a teacher-scholar continues to develop personally and contribute to the field of knowledge.

How this works can be seen, for example, in the area of self-understanding. If a student teacher has had effective guidance in building some depth of self-understanding, she or he, as a teacher, will tend to continue increasing his or her self-knowledge using a wide range of procedures. The gains made, in turn, will increase the teacher's ability to guide youngsters toward self-understanding. Meanwhile the processes—observation, discovery, reflection, and assimilation—on the part of the youngsters as well as the teacher go on with more and more refinements.

The typical study of human development offered teachers, it is said, and often justifiably, is unrelated to real persons in a real world. Consequently, students acquire only someone else's handed-down systematized body of knowledge to which they can neither relate as students nor subsequently as teachers in their own work with human beings. Information about human development and learning should be presented in a way that inspires continuing observation, interpretation, and understanding of particular human beings and of their behavior in teaching-learning encounters.

KNOWLEDGE OF CONTENT TO BE TAUGHT

No one really questions the need for a teacher to know the subject matter he or she is trying to teach. But that is as far as agreement goes, and it is not far enough—the meaning of "know" should be explored further. For a teacher to know the subject matter to be taught is to know it as a discipline—to know the way information about the subject is organized and verified and the methods appropriate to creating new knowledge in the area.

This definition has several useful attributes. First, teaching a discipline is largely dependent upon its structure and methods. The key questions and methods of inquiry used to organize the discipline are the same that serve the student in acquiring knowledge in the subject. Second, knowing the kinds of questions that stimulate further study in a subject and the kinds of methods useful in studying such questions provides the essential bases for continuing to learn in the area. Both teachers and their students should, of course, be striving to learn continually in the discipline. Further, "knowing the subject" in terms of understanding the discipline brings all the excitement of still unanswered questions and of fresh inquiry leading to creative discovery, generates enthusiasm that is communicated without any special effort, and establishes a kind of peer relationship among those who labor in the same field, which often happens with gifted students and their teachers.

KNOWLEDGE OF TEACHING PROCESSES

Teaching itself, apart from accumulated concepts in such undergirding disciplines as psychology, sociology, anthropology, and philosophy, is also a field of study in which knowledge is available, in which special methods of inquiry are definable, and in which teachers should acquire understanding of key questions and the ability to use appropriate methods of inquiry.

Teachers are repeatedly advised to focus on processes as well as products in guiding gifted and talented children. Processes do not operate in a vacuum, of course. They deal with some kind of substance that is determined by a student's needs and interests. But in teacher education programs, a number of key processes, which are of value to all students and particularly those who will work with the gifted, are not sufficiently stressed or employed by teachers of teachers (see Table 3).

Table 3: Key Processes of Teacher Education Programs,

Processes To Be Used or Learned	*Illustrative Activities*
The inductive mode in the discovery and verification of knowledge	Make directed observations of varied groups of persons —describe physical features of age groups —draw hypotheses about physical features of a selected age group —check hypotheses through further observations

Processes To Be Used or Learned   *Illustrative Activities*

—verbalize a possible generalization about observations

—check generalizations with authoritative sources

Discover characteristics of gifted and talented persons

—design an instrument and collect data from individuals representing different kinds of talents

—interview selected teachers who have worked with the gifted to obtain their observations of characteristics

—interview exceptionally gifted persons in the community

—observe several gifted at work (a) (alone) on a project and (b) with a group

—discuss observations with others who have been making similar studies

—from findings of above sources create a list of characteristics of gifted and talented persons

—check the list with those found in the literature

—note similarities and differences; pursue points of difference

Use the college or university class (or workshop or other in-service activity) as a laboratory for studying such concepts as motivation, stimulation, reinforcement, psychological safety, and so on.

—identify when you feel good about what you are asked to do, when you are highly motivated, when you feel proud of yourself—and examine the conditions that brought about your feelings

—share your feelings and the results of your examination with group members, including the teacher

Processes To Be Used or Learned | *Illustrative Activities*

—begin to develop some hunches that might lead to generalizations

—check your hunches repeatedly through self-observation, discussion with group members, what authorities or research findings suggest, and observations of students in a classroom

—use some of your hunches in association with peers or pupils and observe effects

—design and conduct systematic study of one or more major concepts about learning

—test several children to identify their stages in development according to Piaget

Divergent thinking

Brainstorm "far out" ideas for individualizing instruction

Design a game for stimulating children to share their fantasies

—field test the game with two or three different groups

—observe individual differences in the content and fluency of expression among children

Construct a description of the school of the future as you would like to see it

View films (or video tapes) of teaching and identify verbal interactions that

—manifest divergent thinking

—stimulate divergent thinking

Free movement through all cognitive levels (Bloom, 1956), with emphasis on analysis, synthesis, and evaluation

Analyze the emotional climate of a classroom

—describe the characteristics or qualities of the atmosphere

—gather information from participants on their perceptions of the emotional climate and on their observations as

Processes To Be Used or Learned	*Illustrative Activities*
	to what contributes to a "good" emotional climate —identify factors that contribute to or detract from an emotional climate that facilitates freedom to learn
	Prepare a composite of research findings on concept development in young children
	Present a critique of a proposed plan modifying administrative arrangements to provide more effectively for gifted and talented pupils —state criteria to be employed in examination of the plan —gather relevant data —draw conclusions against stated criteria
Consideration of ethical implications	Of recording and filing anecdotal materials on students for future use
	Of invading the privacy of an individual in order to understand behavior under given conditions
	Of a teachers' organization calling a strike
	Of a teacher failing to update subject matter students are expected to learn
Consideration of social implications	Of displaying only perfect papers in a classroom
	Of homogeneous grouping of students for their entire school lives
	Of teachers' tendencies to respond differently to children in terms of their intellectual ability, academic achievement, appearance, family membership, or personality
Use of all categories in Krathwohl's (1964) taxonomy of the affective domain	Examine your own feelings and behavior through several different contacts with intellectually gifted peers to

Processes To Be Used or Learned   *Illustrative Activities*

determine where in the taxonomy your acceptance and respect for each person falls

Design an instructional strategy to help students assess their awareness of how they feel toward persons who differ from them in race, ethnicity, or religion

Locate and field test some of the materials published for use in value clarification

From personal observations of teachers interacting with groups of students define what seem to be manifestations of sensitivity; check observations with literature on sensitivity

Many more processes might be identified and illustrated, but the foregoing is enough to underscore three points that should have more significance in all teacher education programs, especially those educating teachers for work with the gifted. First, individuals learn what they experience. For example, students learn appropriate techniques for problem solving through persuasion and discovery in areas important to them. Second, the very kinds of learning opportunities student teachers are advised to make available for their pupils are equally effective in their own education, including exploring, predicting, relating, taking risks, and creating. Third, student teachers have a right to expect their teachers to exemplify the kinds of teaching behavior they advocate.

Mention should be made of the materials designed to help teachers of teachers in their work. Most are instructional "modules" focusing on a single concept relevant to teaching, such as human variability or reinforcement. If done well, they provide the student and instructor with a concrete body of knowledge, including research findings as well as materials for study, such as films, tapes, or transcripts. The student is guided to selected experiences using the concept, moving from verbalization of the concept through recognizing it in practice, planning to apply it in his or her own behavior, actually using it, and evaluating the consequences. The strategy apparently relies on deductive reasoning, but may be modified to include exercise in inductive reasoning.

TRAINING IN INTELLECTUAL SKILLS

A few skills that have significance for teaching generally and special implications for guiding the gifted merit more attention than they generally receive. Most of what it takes to be a competent teacher is not developed through training, but through education. Nevertheless, there are important skills that are likely to be better developed in practice, and it seems appropriate to speak of "training" in connection with them.

Successful teachers of the gifted, studies show, have certain intellectual styles. They tend to conceptualize, hypothesize, generalize, infer, compare, draw analogies, and so on. Such intellectual processes not only make up a style, they also are skills. Of course, these skills are important for all teachers, since they are directly related to decision making, performance, and evaluation of teaching. Student teachers can be helped to develop such skills by setting expectancies that they will use these skills on a regular basis and by their teachers exhibiting such skills in working with them. Take the skill of hypothesizing, for example. A hypothesis is a hunch about the relationship between two variables. Many teachers' decisions, in fact, are hypotheses that a teaching strategy will produce a specific learning goal. Drawing hunches and systematically testing them in actual situations and collecting and analyzing data are common practices for teachers and part of their responsibility for examining and improving their strategies and materials.

Although skill in hypothesizing is complex and draws upon other skills and relevant knowledge, there are dimensions of the skill that can be identified and on which training can be based. For example, one can learn to identify researchable questions, time the drawing of hunches appropriately, state hypotheses precisely, design techniques and procedures for gathering pertinent information, and analyze and interpret information in relation to the question being investigated and the variables involved.

Opportunities should be provided for student teachers to draw and test hypotheses about relationships between certain of their teaching behaviors and reactions of pupils, about use of certain materials and pupil progress toward achievement of specific objectives, or about relationships between their feeling of confidence in knowing the subject matter and success in teaching a particular concept. Student teachers should be given as much practice in the process as possible, including designing and conducting complete studies of hypotheses.

The skill of drawing inferences is another example. Students should be helped to understand the difference between high- and low-level inferring, the criteria to be met at each level, and when inferring is legitimate and when it is not. In teaching the gifted, it is often noted, teachers should be slow to pronounce judgment and not be judgmental. Teachers who are highly skilled in making inferences are not likely to make judgments without adequate information. They are more likely to test their intuitions and to be sensitive to the feelings of students in sharing their conclusions.

The skills that enable a person to organize, systematize, assimilate, and interrelate information are also important and are especially useful in teaching the gifted. Student teachers should be expected to use these skills regularly, and experiences that guide students in conceptualizing and generalizing should be a daily occurrence. Teachers must not only be able to use such skills, they have to understand them in such a way that they can effectively help others acquire them. Exhibiting them in their own behavior will be one way of teaching others.

TRAINING IN TEACHING SKILLS

Other important skills, called pedagogical skills, relate specifically to teaching. Such skills include leading discussions, asking questions that promote learning, administering diagnostic instruments, giving directions, listening, observing, structuring, reinforcing, and using technical equipment. Student teachers must be helped to understand the different roles these skills play in teaching and to develop competence in their selection and use. Again, practice is the key.

Microteaching is a popular way to practice such skills. A student teacher selects a skill to work on for which a standard of performance has been set, designs a brief teaching situation to last 15 or 20 minutes with a few pupils, and performs the skill while being video taped. Afterward, the teacher, either alone or with a peer or advisor, examines the behavior, and if it does not meet the set of criteria, repeats the sequence until it does.

One danger often associated with microteaching is that students may fail to relate the specific exercise to the whole of teaching. Another is that students may not be able to transfer the skill to complex teaching situations in a real classroom with typical numbers and types of pupils. But such dangers can be avoided by providing the proper context and supplementary experiences.

Technical recording of student teacher performance for analysis can be very useful in skill training, whether microteaching is used or not. For example, taping verbal interactions allows detailed examination of such skills as questioning, giving directions, reinforcing, and so on. Silent film provides data for examination of nonverbal behavior, such as gestures, teacher location in classroom space, and facial expression. Video tape provides both, but it cannot be assumed that the total teaching-learning is recorded even so. After all, a camera records only what it is directed to record. Nevertheless, a program that does not provide student teachers with many opportunities to record, retrieve, and examine their behavior is far from adequate.

The one skill most often overlooked in training teachers is that of observing. It seems to be assumed by their educators that student teachers already possess the skill. Very little direct training is provided in most programs, though students are required to make observations time after time for varied reasons. Students, as well as their mentors, need to study observation theory and techniques, particularly in the area of perceptual psychology, and concentrate on developing skills in observing behavior of pupils, of teaching, and of both in interaction.

There are many instructional units or modules on the market designed to provide training in these skills, published by commercial firms as well as by universities and governmental agencies. Many, for example, are available on questioning techniques, the skills of reinforcement, and the use of technical equipment; a few are now available on building skills in observation. However, there is no reason that educators must turn to commercial products to provide such training. They can design their own units, since training activities that are designed for and used in a specific setting by specific persons are just as effective, if not more so.

A well-developed unit has at least these components: a rationale for the use of the skill, including research evidence where available; procedures for assessing the student as training begins; alternative activities for training, depending upon that assessment; and evaluation of a student's competence following training. A unit should also be validated through considerable field testing prior to its distribution for use.

The three aspects of teacher education—development of self-understanding, acquisition of knowledge, and development of skills—although isolated here for discussion, are obviously interrelated, and a good program for teachers will contain all three. But what insures a good program? It can only be one that is designed to foster competence in each of the three areas.

4

A COMPETENCY-
BASED APPROACH

THE EFFECTIVENESS of a program to educate teachers will depend on the educational climate of the institution offering it, the variety of input behind the design, and whether the curriculum is based on the competencies to be acquired.

The basic premise underlying this book is that the same principles that guide school programs for developing each individual's potential, including the gifted, should also guide programs to educate teachers. This means that teacher education programs should be individualized, that varied opportunities should be available for each student teacher to identify his or her special needs and interests, and that all aspects of the program—the educational climate, teaching strategies, and evaluation criteria—should provide for human differences. Moreover, the designing process should be characterized by continuous inquiry.

It also means that those who teach teachers must themselves possess the attributes, knowledge, and skills essential for facilitating the development of individual potentialities. They are the models with whom their students identify. It has been said that students take on the "culture" of a profession more by osmosis, more by direct continuing contact with professionals, than anything else (Merton, 1957). Culture includes values and attitudes as well as knowledge and skills. It encompasses ways of behaving. That teachers of teachers must be above-average in intelligence, enthusiastic scholars in their specialties, and highly skilled is important. But equally important, if not more so, are personal attributes and predispositions known to be essential in creating a climate conducive to the growth and full development of each person, qualifications desirable for all teachers and critical for those who will work with the gifted.

CREATING THE RIGHT CLIMATE

Studies of how students develop during their college or university years, based on how much their values change, reveal that institutions where most change occurred have certain characteristics in common. Relationships between students and faculty were close; it was expected that ideas would be questioned, differences of opinion would be examined, and persons would be held accountable for their decisions; the instructional strategies emphasized dialogue, discussion, debate, and inquiry (Astin, 1977). The institutional ethos—the unspoken, unwritten understandings—set expectancies, and students responded to them. In fact, all members of a community do.

Faculty members in an institution, as well as students in a class, teachers in a school, and pupils in a classroom tend to do what they perceive "important others" expect. When it is expected, from the top down, that individuals will constantly engage in improving their knowledge and skills, most will. When it is expected that individuals will be flexible and open to new ideas and will respect each person for what he or she is and can become, most will.

Reward systems play a dominant role in setting expectancies. Yet in higher education institutions there is sometimes quite a gap between what decision makers say is important and what they do in the way of distributing rewards. In such cases expectancies are inferred from the reward practices, rather than from what is said. If the system fails to recognize and reward program development activities, most faculty members will resist studying programs and making changes in them.

As it stands today, few faculty are prepared to design an effective program or curriculum for teaching teachers. Only rarely does faculty apprenticeship include attention to the study of, or practice in, college teaching or of program designing. As a result, higher education personnel tend to perceive their roles primarily as producers of knowledge in their own field of specialization. Contributing further to their lack of preparedness is the almost complete absence of supervision, in-service education, or staff development practices. Add to this current budgetary limitations, and it is clear that very special steps will have to be taken if higher education personnel are to devote time and resources to making the changes needed in programs of teacher education.

Setting the right climate and expectancies for student teachers necessitates dramatic changes in professorial behavior and administrative posture. If any real change is to occur, faculty members will have to be encouraged and rewarded for re-educating themselves and for assigning high priority to program examination and designing. Specific opportunities need to be available for faculty to study schools, to analyze proposals advanced by educational authorities, to carry on their own investigations as well as analyze others' research, and to reflect on these in terms of self-examination and improvement. The notion that only educators at the lower levels need continuing in-service education is invalid and should be abandoned. Every educator needs the stimulation and the opportunity to engage in continuous recreating of the personal and professional self.

INPUT FROM ALL LEVELS

When it comes to designing programs, more and more emphasis is being given to cooperation between lower schools and higher education. The standards currently used by the National Council for Accreditation of Teachers Education (1976) include several instances in which personnel from schools and higher education institutions must cooperate in designing, conducting, and evaluating programs at both pre-service and advanced levels. The guidelines adopted by the Council for Exceptional Children in 1976 are equally specific:

The planning and implementation of special education programs should include opportunities at all levels for input from all constituent groups, including the consumer, affected by the planning. (p. 17)

Preparation programs should reflect and promote the kind of interprofessional cooperation that should occur in school programs. (p. 12)

The involvement of all constituent groups is critical. Appropriate, effective, and creative program designing is far more likely to result from a combination of the special kinds of expertise each group brings to the task.

Furthermore, unless there is continuing and close contact between school programs and programs of teacher preparation, the chances are great that both schools and colleges will be losers. School personnel run the risk of missing out on newly validated practices that could be put rapidly into programs and the new knowledge that higher education personnel may have contributed to research, experimentation, and staff development. On the other side, without the input of school personnel and continuing contact with what goes on in schools and communities, higher education faculty frequently lose touch with reality and fail to incorporate into their teaching the practical dimensions along with the theoretical. It is helpful to think of teacher education as a system within a system (see Figure 3) that includes state agencies and accreditation agencies as well as higher education, schools, and local communities.

STEPS IN THE PROCESS

All steps in the process—designing, conducting, evaluating—should be considered simultaneously rather than one step at a time. Evaluation reports are all too often left to gather dust, their findings unreflected upon and unused. And all too often elaborate programs are designed without full consideration of how the design can be put into operation or how its effectiveness can be evaluated. Failure to conceptualize the processes of designing as one continuing, unbroken spiral (see Figure 4) accounts for much of the disappointment and lack of success experienced in efforts to bring about change in educational programs.

It is not only the failure to relate the steps simultaneously that prevents success; it is also the failure to take into account the potential impact of a decision about one component on the program as a whole. For example, a decision to modularize one or more components without considering both the resources

Figure 3: The Teacher Education System—A System within a System

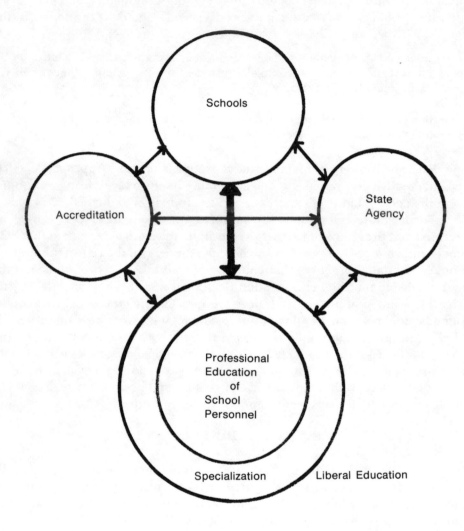

Figure 4: An On-going Continuing Process

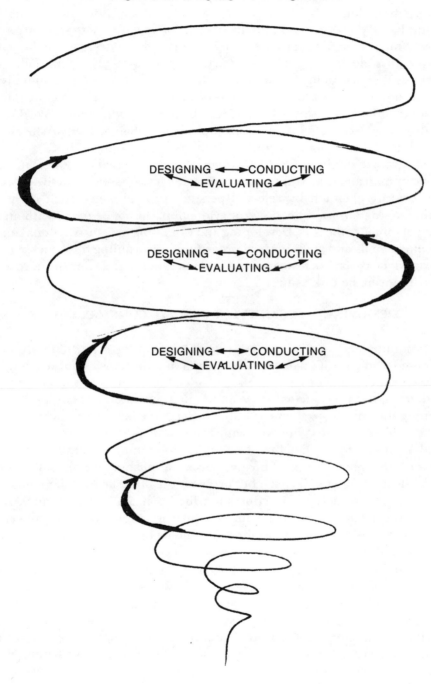

needed to develop modules and the readiness of faculty and students to use them effectively may ultimately lead to failure of the plan. Or a decision to move a large number of professors out into the schools for activities with student teachers may come to naught because of the failure of program designers to be sensitive to the possible threat to professors who may be insecure about their own ability to deal with practical situations in the schools. Or a decision to individualize one or more program components may fail simply because neither faculty nor students know how to individualize activities or modify their record keeping to draw the necessary individualized profiles of their students. The ripple effect of a decision can touch a multitude of areas (see Figure 5).

Program designing, of course, cannot be accomplished without allocating adequate human and material resources. Specific tasks, essential to the process, require priority attention by selected persons. Crucial steps, such as needs assessment, program modifications, or evaluation, cannot be made without assigning personnel to the task. Developing and validating new instructional materials require funds and staff. Revised procedures for profiling and tracking students cannot be designed, tested, or put into operation unless one or more individuals are given the task as first priority.

DESIGNING A COMPETENCY-BASED CURRICULUM

Programs and courses for educating teachers have traditionally been based on conceptions of goals for schools and assumptions about teaching in relation to achievement of those goals. The idea that education should prepare teachers to perform designated roles and to demonstrate their competence in performing those roles is a theme running through the history of teacher education. The models may vary, but the theme is the same (see Figure 6). Essentially the model is a systems model, that is, designers have in mind some "ends" that determine to a large degree the "means" for accomplishing the ends. Disagreements relate not to the model itself but to the nature of the goals and means and to the degree of openness or closedness ascribed to it. The model may be misused. But in spite of narrow or incomplete interpretations by some educators and ill-advised rushing into plans, the model holds up. It forms the basis of the current movement toward a competency-based curriculum.

The approach to designing such a curriculum is three-fold. It is systematic, it is process oriented, and it is situationally based.

Systematic means that the curriculum is seen as one subsystem in relation to others in increasingly larger systems, a point stressed earlier. It also means that the design proceeds from definition of desired outcomes and that the substance of the curriculum (both content and processes) is directly relevant to the desired outcomes. And, as stated earlier, it means continual inquiry into the effects of all components and constant feedback into all parts of the system of

Figure 5: The Ripple Effects of Decisions on Decisions

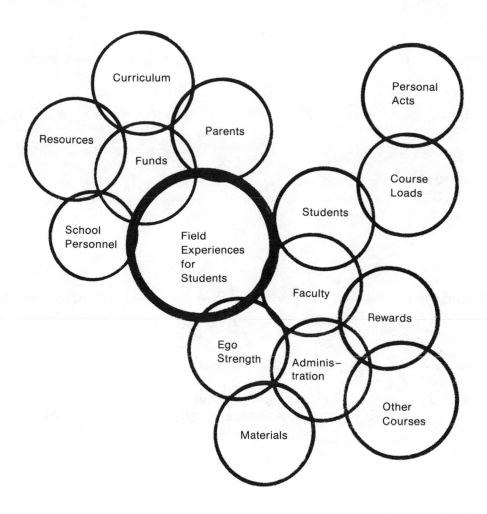

Figure 6: Models for Curriculum Designing

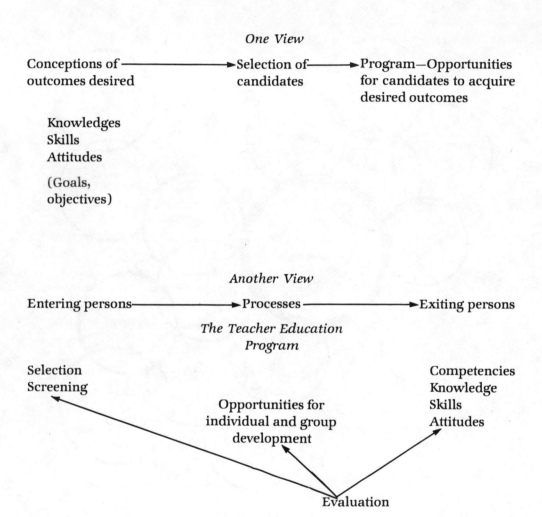

One View

Conceptions of ————————► Selection of ————► Program—Opportunities
outcomes desired   candidates   for candidates to acquire
                                                        desired outcomes

Knowledges
Skills
Attitudes

(Goals,
objectives)

Another View

Entering persons ——————————► Processes ——————————► Exiting persons

*The Teacher Education
Program*

Selection   Competencies
Screening   Knowledge
                    Opportunities for   Skills
                    individual and group   Attitudes
                    development

                            Evaluation

what is learned by the inquiry. In this sense, the system is always open ended, never static, and always responding to new information and conditions (see Figure 6).

Process oriented means simply that the approach is focused on specific processes rather than specific content. For example, it requires designers to identify the general outcomes they desire, but does not dictate what the specific outcomes shall be; it requires selecting and sequencing of alternative learning experiences in relation to the stated outcomes, but does not require any particular learning experiences. It identifies the processes required, but not the hoped-for products.

Once the approach is systematic and process oriented, it will automatically be situationally centered, that is, designed by groups of persons in a given setting, not something developed elsewhere and borrowed, but directly related to particular factors and forces in a special setting.

This approach has been criticized, but always the criticism is misplaced. For example, if program designers choose to identify two thousand minute items of behavior as objectives rather than broad goals, that is the shortcoming of the designers, not of the approach. Similarly, if designers choose to evaluate only what can be quantified and measured as outcomes, that too is the fault of the designers, not of the approach. And if some designers limit their outcomes to specific cognitive objectives and fail to include personal characteristics, predispositions, and attitudes, that is the designers' misreading of what a competency-based curriculum is. Finally, if some curriculum designers let stated goals close their minds to new and exciting possibilities beyond their goals, that is the result of the designers' rigidity, not the shortcomings in the approach.

What are the main procedures in such an approach? Four basic steps have been generally agreed upon:

1. Define the knowledge, skills, and attitudes, in short, the competencies to be achieved
2. Design alternative strategies for helping different students achieve them
3. Evaluate the degree to which they do achieve them
4. Feedback the results into all elements of the system.

The four steps have a sequential relationship to one another, yet each step involves consideration of the others in terms of the total context. In fact, program designers, in light of their own styles and situations, may enter into the sequence at any point. For example, some may prefer to deal with step two first and propose various strategies before asking why or what justifies the proposal. Others may find it more productive to begin by evaluating a present program or activity and then consider possible goals and strategies. To recognize the sequential nature of the four steps does not mandate a closed system nor a rigid sequence nor a narrow consideration of each step alone.

IDENTIFYING TEACHING COMPETENCIES*

The identification of competencies depends on the nature and goals of education in a particular setting and the roles given teachers in that setting. Studies of teacher roles, including their personal and social values and attitudes and drawing heavily upon reported empirical evidence about practice, are available, making it possible to translate educational goals into effective teacher roles and into the competencies and behaviors essential to performing those roles. Such translations, however, are theoretical, because they require intellectual leaps over important gaps in knowledge and need to be subjected continually to further analysis and to tests of validity and practicality in the real world. Note the space given to assumptions in identifying competencies, illustrated by Figure 7.

Another approach to identifying competencies involves gathering many descriptions of teacher behavior, subjecting these descriptions to analysis, synthesis, and evaluation, and finally abstracting sets of behaviors that make up teaching competencies. The danger here lies in reducing the complex act of

Figure 7: Identifying Competencies

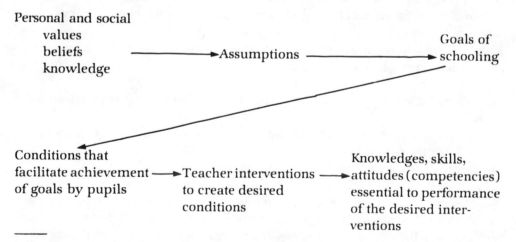

*Portions of this discussion are adapted from Lindsey, M. Competency-based education: Historical, current, and future perspectives. In *Competency-based education: Theory, practice, evaluation.* Athens: University of Georgia, College of Education, Department of Curriculum and Supervision, 1975, pp. 1–38.

teaching to performance alone and arriving at statements of preferred performances rather than competencies based on a range of relevant knowledge, values, and attitudes. To put it another way, if a competent teacher is expected to *know* and to *feel* as well as to *do*, program planning will depend on more than descriptions of teacher behavior in interactions with students in classrooms.

Program designers may begin with a particular curriculum and then determine what knowledge, skills, and attitudes are essential to implement it. Or they may begin with a learning theory and use that to define the competencies needed. Or they may begin with a discipline and use that to determine the competencies teachers need to help students master the discipline. Any of these approaches may initiate the planning, but it should be remembered they are partial steps and should be placed in the whole context suggested by Figure 7.

Perhaps the best approach is to be guided by a conception of the wholeness of the person. If there is any unifying force, it is the person; if unity is to be achieved at all, it must occur in the human being. This approach suggests that outcomes to be achieved by students or teachers might be categorized in the three areas — what a teacher needs to be, to know, and to be able to do. Having the person as the unifying element in program designing provides for continuity also. A person is always in a state of becoming, always needs and wants more knowledge, and always needs and wants to increase competence in performance. Continuity for the person occurs when these needs are met, as they come and go, ebb and flow, in a maturing individual. Continuity in programs for teachers is provided by constantly refining and modifying conceptions of a teacher's need to be, to know, and to do, and in the creation of learning opportunities relevant to those needs.

With this approach in mind, it is possible to take current programs as points of departure and to improve them significantly by asking how each component contributes to:

> The development of those characteristics and qualities essential to effective guidance of gifted youngsters?
> The acquisition of knowledge required?
> The development of intellectual and pedagogical skills required?

For example, it is appropriate to ask what kinds of contributions liberal education should make to a student teacher's becoming, knowing, and doing as a professional. Do the kinds of experiences most students have in liberal education actually facilitate development of the intellectual skills needed to work with the gifted? In what ways do they help develop ego strength or respect, trust, and love of fellow human beings? In what ways do they contribute to the development of teaching skills?

The identical questions need to be asked of those components usually called "specializations" or "majors." All too commonly this is an accumulation of courses in which content becomes increasingly narrow at advanced stages and in which students have little opportunity to deal with the central organizing structure or to use the methods of the discipline. This too must be changed.

But the weakest component at present is the one that deals specifically with the study of education—schools, teaching, how human beings develop and learn, teaching practice, and internship. Of all components it fails the most to provide students with experiences that will contribute to the personal and professional characteristics, knowledge, and skills essential for teachers who have gifted students in their class. Here, if nowhere else in a program, student teachers should be experiencing the processes they are being urged to use with their pupils when they become teachers. Here, more than any place else in a program, they ought to be in contact with excellence in professional practice.

It is often argued that changes in programs must begin with what is and work toward what ought to be, course by course. Instead, what is urged here is to examine the value of broad components—liberal education, subject matter specialization, and professional education. Course by course approaches tend to militate against unity and continuity. But unity and continuity in programs can be provided by examining the three areas of what a person needs to be, to know, and to do to be effective with gifted youngsters. To revise the entire program of undergraduate teachers' education in an ongoing college or university may be unrealistic, but such an approach does lend itself to the study and revision of at least the professional components in situations where adequate controls can be exercised. A broken-front approach, that is working on a program piece by piece, still has far reaching implications, especially since modifications in any part of a program (a subsystem) will have an impact on other parts of the whole system.

Whatever approach or combination of approaches is employed, a critical question concerns the "bodies of knowledge" used in defining competencies. Considerably more attention than is now the case needs to be given to those disciplines that help in understanding and interpreting individual and group behavior and to those that contribute to the principles and methods of decision making in teaching. Failure to draw upon relevant strategies from such disciplines as sociology, anthropology, psychology, and philosophy when identifying competencies may result in lists of teaching behaviors limited to a craft rather than a profession.

A frequent mistake is the weight attached to measurable competencies. If a set of behaviors seems desirable on the basis of reason and observation, it ought to be included whether ways to measure it are available or not. Then deliberate effort should be made during the entire process of designing, conducting, and evaluating the program to build ways of validating the competency and of assessing its presence or absence in teacher behavior.

Some lists of teacher competencies that have appeared contain so much detail—the items number in the hundreds—that a desirable wholeness may be lost in a mass of unrelated bits and pieces. Dangers also lurk in the interpretations that students, practicing teachers, and university personnel make of such lists and the implications they draw from them. For example, the number of listed competencies may be unreal for any single person to achieve; they may be viewed as rigid, inflexible, and prescriptive; and they may be interpreted as denying personal style in teaching. Program designers should arrive at a reasonable number of important competencies, each stated at a relatively high level of abstraction, and then develop a range of alternative behaviors relevant to each competency, keeping such constellations open ended for input by creative students and teachers according to their personal styles and experiences in diverse settings.

Because all other stages in planning, conducting, and evaluating the program rest squarely on the competencies identified, this phase of designing is perhaps the most critical. It is also a public statement expressing a basic point of view and commitment.

DESIGNING INSTRUCTION STRATEGIES

When a teaching competency has been identified, the alternative behaviors relevant to it defined, and the competency validated to the extent possible, the next question is how the competency will be taught. The question has four parts (see Figure 8). What is the present status of the student teacher in respect to the competency? What conditions will facilitate the student's progress toward achievement of the competency? What interventions by the teacher will generate those conditions? How can achievement of the competency be determined?

The first and last questions of assessment and evaluation are important in designing instruction. One cannot design instructional strategies for a given student without reference to what he or she already knows and can do. One cannot ignore the final evaluation of a student's competence without losing vital feedback, possibly wasting human and material resources, and risking boredom or rejection by the student.

Adequate evidence is not now available to validate many of the predictions and assumptions on which teachers of teachers depend in designing instruction. Where evidence is available, it ought to be used. Where it is unavailable, educators should systematically seek to contribute it. Continuing investigation into all components of the instructional system and feedback into all its parts, the hallmark of an open system, promise to hasten the day when decisions can be based on more firm predictions. The need for teacher educators to expand their knowledge base for instructional decisions by systematic inquiry cannot be overemphasized.

Figure 8: Designing Instruction

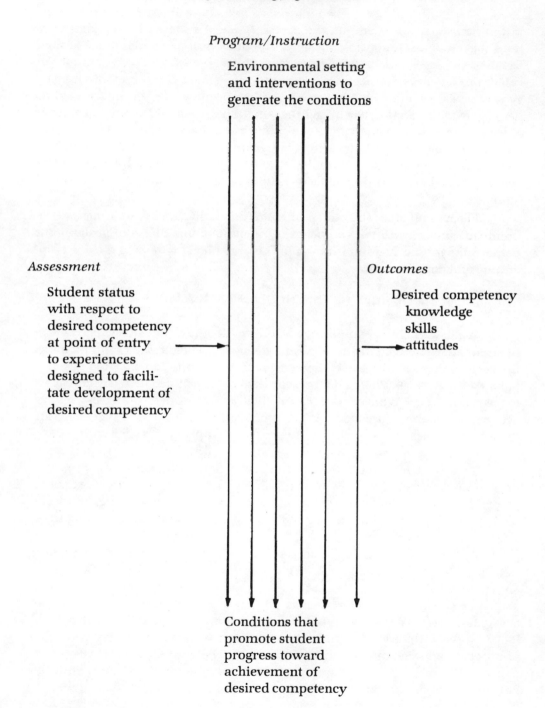

Program/Instruction

Environmental setting
and interventions to
generate the conditions

Assessment

Student status
with respect to
desired competency
at point of entry
to experiences
designed to facili-
tate development of
desired competency

Outcomes

Desired competency
knowledge
skills
attitudes

Conditions that
promote student
progress toward
achievement of
desired competency

QUESTIONS OF CRITERIA AND EVALUATION

Evaluating a competency-based teacher education program is a large task encompassing many and diverse activities. But first, it should be asked, what is being evaluated? Is it the design? The operation? Or the consequences for graduates? All three aspects—the design, the operation, and the consequences —need to be evaluated if program evaluation is to be complete. Further, the evaluation of any one aspect should, where appropriate, inform the evaluation and planning of the other two aspects.

To judge the consequences of any feature of a program will depend on evidence that the feature believed to be operative was in fact existent. For example, it is pointless to ask how effective a program was in producing teachers with creative individual styles if nothing in the program was geared to that outcome and, in fact, the opposite was actually the case—students were made to conform. Again, if graduates are unable to manage a classroom, did the program provide opportunities for students to manage a real classroom? When consequences are evaluated, there must be adequate data on the actual operation of the program, the opportunities provided, and the standards of excellence set before drawing conclusions about possible relationships.

The following criteria, which describe a competency-based teacher education (CBTE) program, are the result of extended deliberation and substantial testing in ongoing programs (Burke et al., 1974). Readers may disagree with certain specifics summarized here, but in general the criteria can serve as guidelines for designing and appraising competency-based programs.

Competency Specifications

Competencies are based on an analysis of the professional roles and theoretical responsibilities.

Competencies—knowledge, skills, and attitudes—are described in terms of outcomes expected.

Competency statements are a realistic criterion for assessment.

Competencies are treated as tentative predictors of professional effectiveness and subject to continual validation.

The competencies specified are made public.

Graduates are expected to demonstrate a wide range of competencies.

Instruction

The instructional program is derived from, and linked to, specified competencies.

Instruction is organized into units of manageable size to develop competency, accommodate learner style, sequence preference, pacing, and perceived needs.

Progress is determined by demonstrated competence, and the extent of learner's progress is made known to him or her throughout the program. Instructional specifications are reviewed and revised on the basis of feedback.

Assessment

Assessment of competency measures is related to valid demonstration of defined competency standards.

Assessments are specific, realistic, and sensitive to nuance.

Assessment is manageable and useful in decision making.

Assessment standards are specified and made public.

Governance and Management

Policy statements, in broad outline, are written to govern the intended structure, content, operation, and resource base of the program.

Management functions, responsibilities, procedures, and mechanisms are clearly defined and made explicit.

Total Program

Program staff attempt overall to enhance the attitudes and behaviors desired of students in the program.

Provisions are made for staff orientation, assessment, improvement, and reward.

Research and dissemination activities are an integral part of the total instructional system.

Institutional flexibility is sufficient for all aspects of the program.

The program is planned and operated as a totally unified, integrated system.

The criteria, however, leave untouched some important considerations in designing programs. Balance is one. Balance does not mean equal parts, equal weight, or equal amounts. It refers instead to appropriate relationships between desired outcomes for the student teacher and learning opportunities in a program. As the guidelines adopted by the Council for Exceptional Children (1976) show (see Table 4), several kinds of balance are important.

Another consideration is emphasis or focus. For example, does the total design include appropriate emphasis on the higher cognitive processes, on the development of the very special personal characteristics essential to work with the gifted, on facilitating the teacher behaviors known to be effective, and on

Table 4:   Guidelines for Achieving Balance

Preparation programs should provide balance between special and general educational skills to develop in each practitioner both the unique competency to function in special roles and the ability to contribute appropriately to the planning and implementation of a variety of programs for exceptional as well as all other individuals.

In addition to balance in general and special education, balance in such other matters as these is important:

Freedom for the student teacher to select goals, design his/her activities, determine assessment.	Restrictions or prescriptions of minimum requirements in terms of goals, experiences, and assessment
Independent, self-selected learning activities	Instructor- (or counselor-) selected and guided learning activities
Field-based activities	Campus-based activities
Individual activities	Group activities
Seminar-type experiences	Formal course experiences
Exploring, expanding, discovering for the self or with peers	Organizing, systematizing, and assimilating others' ideas (p. 19)

opportunities to work directly with gifted children and to study one's own behavior in such direct contact?

Form and function and the relationship between the two are also useful considerations for the curriculum designer. Is the intent (function) of the design explicit? Is its form (structure) specifically relevant to its intent?

Criteria, then, becomes a many-sided question, with ripple effects on evaluation. However, a few basic questions may serve as a compass for direction. If teacher education programs are to illustrate the principles advocated for programs for the gifted and if a competency-based approach is appropriate for all teachers who will work with the gifted, either in a regular classroom or as specialists, then the following questions may help steer the way, either in designing or evaluating programs for the education of teachers of the gifted.

Basic Criteria for Assessing the Quality of Teacher Education Programs

Are the goals of the program made explicit?

Are the goals of the program derived from conceptions of teacher roles and the knowledge, skills, and attitudes (competencies) essential to competent performance of those roles? Do the goals take into account the values and purposes of schools in a democracy? Do they reflect the special requirements of gifted persons? Are they stated in such a way as to provide direction for designing, conducting, and evaluating?

*Are the opportunities the program provides for students
consistent with the stated goals?*

Is provision made for each student teacher to assess his or her status with respect to stated goals? Does the program offer enough alternatives for each student to select those experiences best suited to him or her? Are periodic student evaluations based on stated goals? Does the total program encompass all goals? Has the program been analyzed to detect duplication, omission, or obsolescence in terms of goals? Has such analysis resulted in modifications?

Is the program dynamic rather than static?

Does the program have built-in evaluation and feedback? Is systematic inquiry (research) an integral part? Is the information gained used to modify where change is suggested? Is the program regularly compared with new knowledge, research, and theoretical propositions coming from the outside?

Are those who design and operate the program effective models?

Do university or college personnel exhibit the characteristics wanted in teachers who guide gifted and talented youngsters? Do they challenge student teachers to do their best, manifest respect for individuality, and stimulate creativity? Are they scholarly or thoroughly engaged in respect to their specialties, to the education of the gifted, and to teaching? Are they up to date, enthusiastic, and creative in their own work? Do they share their enterprises with students? Are they in regular contact with persons, schools, and programs where education of gifted and talented youngsters is going on? Do they continually evaluate their own performance, using data from a range of sources, including students?

*Are those who have a stake in the program significantly involved
in its designing, implementation, and evaluation?*

Are those in, or related to, the field in any way regularly involved in planning the program? Has a needs assessment been made of appropriate groups, individuals, and agencies? Are student teachers and graduates involved in planning? Are specialists in education of the gifted involved in the preparation of regular teachers, in other dimensions?

Are adequate resources available and productively used?

Does the faculty encompass the breadth and depth of specialties needed? Is it of sufficient size to provide students with various points of view, styles, and specialties? Are the loads of faculty members reasonable, taking into account responsibilities in teaching, personal-professional study, laboratory activities in the field, contributions to professional associations, institutional citizenship obligations, and so on?

Is adequate space available for productive work by faculty and students? Are library holdings up to date, of quality and scope, and easily accessible? Are technical equipment and assistance available when needed?

Does the institutional environment stimulate expectancies and achievement?

Are student teachers as well as faculty respected and liked? Do persons feel secure, accepted, and trusted? Are individuals encouraged to develop their full potentialities? Does the reward system foster individual development? Do standards for work by faculty, students, and administrators require excellence? Is it expected that programs will be subjected to examination and revision on a regular basis? Is program development perceived as an important responsibility of all in the institutional community?

Does the program provide continuity between practice and theory?

Does the program involve a student teacher early and continuously in practice experience with the education of the gifted? Does the involvement include specific clinical, laboratory, and practice activities? Is a student's experience in the field or laboratory so guided as to deepen his or her understanding through related reading, discussion, conferring, and reflecting? Is there a continuous flow between practice and experience-grounded conceptualizing about practice? Does the program provide for student experience in different teaching approaches and styles in a range of situations where the needs of the gifted, among others, are identified and nurtured?

Does the program provide both social and independent experience?

Is each student involved long enough in a group of peers and professionals to develop selfhood and skills that may not be developed individually in isolation from others? Is each student also expected to carry on independent study, using his or her own style and creativity to the best advantage, on a continuing basis?

REFERENCES

Astin, A. *Four critical years: Effects of college on beliefs, attitudes, and knowledge.* San Francisco: Jossey-Bass, 1977.

Benjamin, S. *Table of state certification for teachers of the gifted.* Scarsdale, NY: 1978. Unpublished study.

Bloom, B.S., et al. *Taxonomy of educational objectives: Cognitive domain.* New York: David McKay, 1956.

Bokee, M., Office of Gifted and Talented Education. Personal communication, December 20, 1979.

Bruch, K, et al. Current degree programs in gifted education. *Gifted Child Quarterly,* 1977, *21,* 141–153.

Burke, J.B., et al. *Criteria for describing and assessing competency-based programs.* Syracuse, NY: Multistate Consortium, James Collins, Coordinator, Syracuse University, 1974.

Combs, A.W., Aliva, D.L., & Purkey, W.W. *Helping relationships: Basic concepts for the helping professions.* Boston: Allyn & Bacon, 1971. pp. 39–43.

Council for Exceptional Children. *Guidelines for personnel in the education of exceptional children.* Reston, VA: The Council, 1976.

Curry, J.B., & Sato, I.S. Training on the right track. *Gifted Child Quarterly,* Summer 1977, *21* (2), 200.

Gold, M.J. *Education of the intellectually gifted.* Columbus, OH: Merrill, 1965, pp. 412–413.

Grant, B.M. Revised proposed plan designed by William Paterson College representatives at the National/State Leadership Training Institute on Gifted and Talented. Paterson, NJ: The William Paterson College, Department of Education, 1978.

Guilford, J.P. *The nature of human intelligence.* New York: McGraw-Hill, 1967.

Krathwohl, D.R., et al. *Taxonomy of educational objectives: Handbook 2: Affective domain.* New York: David McKay, 1964.

Maeroff, G. University aids gifted junior high students. *New York Times,* May 22, 1979.

Maker, C.J. *Training teachers for the gifted and talented: A comparison of models.* Reston, VA: ERIC Clearinghouse on Handicapped and Gifted Children, Council for Exceptional Children, 1975.

Marland, S.P., Jr. *Education of the gifted and talented* (Vol. 1). Report to the Congress of the United States by the U.S. Commissioner of Education. Washington, D.C.: U.S. Department of Health, Education, and Welfare, 1971.

Marland, S.P., Jr. Our gifted and talented children—A priceless national resource. *Intellect,* October 1972, 16–19.

Merton, R. *Student physician.* New York: Columbia University, Bureau of Applied Social Research, 1957.

National Council for Accreditation of Teacher Education. *Standards for accreditation.* Washington, D.C.: The Council, 1976.

Nelson, J.B., & Cleland, D. L. *The role of the teacher of gifted and creative children.* In W.B.

Barbe & J.S. Renzulli (Eds.), *Psychology and education of the gifted*. New York: Halsted Press, 1975, p. 441.

North Carolina State Department of Public Instruction. *Competency-based program for certification—Gifted and talented* (Rev. ed.). Raleigh: 1976, pp. 1, 3.

North Carolina State Education Department. *College/university courses approved for gifted and talented*. Raleigh: 1976.

Renzulli, J.S. Instructional management systems: A model for organizing and developing in-service training workshops. *Gifted Child Quarterly*, 1977, *21*, 186–87.

Stanley, J.C., Keating, D.P., & Fox, L.H. (Eds.). *Mathematical talent: Discovery, description, and development*. Baltimore: Johns Hopkins Press, 1974.

Taba, H., Levine, S., & Elzey, F.F. *Thinking in elementary school children* (U.S.O.E. Cooperative Research Project No. 1574). San Francisco: San Francisco State College, 1964.

University of Georgia, College of Education, Department of Educational Psychology. *Graduate programs in education of the gifted*. Athens: 1977, pp. 1–4.

Williams, F.E. Models for encouraging creativity in the classroom. In J.C. Gowan & E.P. Torrance (Eds.), *Educating the ablest*, Itasca, IL: F.E. Peacock, 1971, p. 230.

ANNOTATED BIBLIOGRAPHY

TEACHER EDUCATION PROGRAMS

Bruch, K. Current degree programs in gifted education. *Gifted Child Quarterly*, 1977, 22, 141–153.

> This program information was compiled by graduate students in gifted education at the University of Georgia.

Burke, B., Hansen, J., Houston, R., & Johnson, C. *Criteria for describing and assessing competency-based programs.* Syracuse, NY: Multistate Consortium, Syracuse University, 1974.

Council for Exceptional Children. *Guidelines for personnel in the education of exceptional children: Professional standards and guidelines project.* Reston, VA: 1976.

> The Council for Exceptional Children suggests processes by which agents of teacher preparation might make decisions on personnel recruitment, curriculum, and methods of instruction within their preparation programs. Although the focus is on special education of the handicapped, the approach shows the direction in which these agencies might move in preparing teachers of the gifted.

Crandall, D.P. Training and supporting linking agents. In N. Nash & J. Culbertson (Eds.), *Linking processes in educational improvement: Concepts and applications.* Columbus, OH: University Council for Educational Administration, 1977.

> Schools can only be changed by people, people familiar with and trained to draw on the appropriate resources. Crandall describes an organization that selects and trains people to use systematic problem-solving to achieve change within a school system.

Curry, J., & Sato, I.S. Training on the right track. *Gifted Child Quarterly*, 1977, 21, 200–204.

> Curry and Sato state the principles behind training as conducted by the National/State Leadership Training Institute on the Gifted and Talented.

David, W. J., & Fairchild, M.R. A study of noncategorical teacher preparation in special education: A self realization model. *Exceptional Child*, 1976, 2, 390–397.

> An initial, condensed report of a two-year study on undergraduate teacher preparation in special education. It compares a new approach, which is noncategorical and competency based and uses extended field activities, with a more traditional method. Data were collected for experimental and control groups in the areas of attitudes, self-concept, knowledge in special education, and teaching performance. Where significant differences emerged, they often favored the control group. Data judged more specific to the project goals were significantly higher for the experimental subjects. These data and student interest formed the basis for program modifications and a continuation of the new approach.

Dunkin, M., & Biddle, B. *The study of teaching.* New York: Holt, Rinehart, and Winston, 1974.

> Discusses principles of teaching, educational research in teaching, and the training of teachers.

Feldhusen, J. Practicum activities for students and gifted children in a university course. *Gifted Child Quarterly*, 1973, 17, 124–129.

> Presents a description of the goals and activities of a course "Gifted, Creative, and Talented Children" taught by Dr. Feldhusen at Purdue University. The course fits a three tiered model: At State 1 knowledge and understanding is transmitted; State 2 instructional activities emphasize analysis, synthesis, and evaluation; at State 3 the focus is on using knowledge and abilities in dealing with the real-life situations.

Fox, L., & Tobin, D. A summer institute for teachers on mathematical talent. *Intellectually Talented Youth Bulletin,* 1978, *4.*

> One example of a summer institute, or workshop, descriptions of which appear in this bulletin from time to time. It is part of a larger program for study of and development of "Mathematically Precocious Youth."

French, J.L. The preparation of teachers of the gifted. *Journal of Teacher Education,* 1961, *12,* 69–72.

> This article from the early 60s describing the objectives and giving outlines of college courses on the gifted suggests that not much has changed.

Gear, G.H. Effects of training on teacher's accuracy in the identification of gifted children. *Gifted Child Quarterly,* 1978, *22,* 90–97.

> Training did improve the effectiveness of teacher referrals of intellectually gifted students in a rural population. This improved effectiveness was accomplished without any loss of efficiency.

Gordon, T.E. *Teacher effectiveness training.* New York: Peter Wyden, 1974.

Gross, N., Giacquinta, J.B., & Bernstein, M. *Implementing organizational innovations.* New York: Basic Books, 1971.

> This case study reveals some of the factors that inhibit the implementation of change in the elementary schools.

Harris, B.M., & Bessent, W. *In-service education: A guide to better practice.* Englewood Cliffs, NJ: Prentice-Hall, 1969.

> Describes an approach to in-service that is highly experiential in nature involving the lab technique and problem-solving activities.

Hill, M.B. *Enrichment programs for intellectually gifted pupils.* Sacramento: California State Department of Education (Project Talent), 1969.

> Contains a brief review of the in-service program for this California project. The program included topical sessions in a specific sequence, workshops, and observation lessons. There is a good concise section on the purpose of teacher training.

Houston, W.R. (Ed.), *Exploring competency based education.* Chicago: Science Research Association, 1972.

> An exceptionally clear account of the progress, problems, and prospects of CBTE by evaluating the pros and cons.

Isaacs, A.F. Preparation for teachers of the gifted. In E.P. Torrance & J.C. Gowan, *Educating the ablest.* New York: Peacock Publishers, 1971, p. 69.

> The importance of training courses for gifted education are ranked by administrators, teachers, and state departments of certification.

Joyce, B., & Weil, M. *Models of teaching.* Englewood Cliffs, NJ: Prentice-Hall, 1972.

> Included are approximately 20 possible approaches to or patterns of teaching. A knowledge of the various models can help a teacher choose an approach appropriate to a particular situation or a particular group of children.

Laird, A.W., & Kowalski, C.J. Survey of 1564 colleges and universities on courses offered in the education of the gifted-teacher training. *Gifted Child Quarterly,* 1972, *16,* 93–111.

> A thorough report on the state of pre-service teacher education in the area of the gifted in the early 70s. Tables indicate which universities have offerings in this area as well as which universities would like to begin or expand programs.

Maker, J.C. *Training teachers for the gifted and talented: A comparison of models.* Reston, VA: Council for Exceptional Children, 1975.

Reviews the literature on characteristics of teachers of the gifted and on programs that provide training for teachers. Competency-based teacher education is discussed in relation to gifted education.

Newland, T.E. *The gifted in socioeducational perspective.* Englewood Cliffs, NJ: Prentice-Hall, 1976.

Provides a comprehensive and detailed examination of strategies and programs for the gifted. Socio-psychological factors that can encourage the gifted child are described. Implications for teacher training are discussed.

Renzulli, J.S. Instructional management systems: A model for organizing and developing in-service training workshops. *Gifted Child Quarterly*, 1977, *21*, 186–195.

Outlines an organized workshop approach that will prove more effective than the usual one-shop in-service workshop.

Rockefeller, D.C. *Coming to our senses: The arts, education, and Americans Panel.* New York: McGraw-Hill, 1977.

Provides a comprehensive view of the arts in American schools. Model programs in each art discipline are presented. Teachers and administrators are given recommendations as to procedures for facilitating artistic expression.

Sarason, S.B. *The culture of the school and the problem of change.* Boston: Allyn & Bacon, 1971.

Examines the question of why, in a school system, the more things change, the more they remain the same. Chapter 8, in particular, focuses on the complexity of the role of the teacher.

Shaffer, V.F., & Troutt, G.E., Jr. Courses offered on the education of the gifted. *Gifted Child Quarterly*, 1970, *14*, 8–23.

An earlier report on pre-service education for teachers of the gifted.

Sisk, D. Teaching the gifted and talented teacher: A training model. *Gifted Child Quarterly*, 1975, *19*, 179–184.

Describes the thorough and detailed training program at the University of South Florida (Tampa). The program includes work in four major areas: the progressional, the specialization, the liberal arts, and field work. It is implemented through small group dynamics, apprentice-type field work, modeling, and community impact involvement. An intensive five-week summer program is also described.

Torrance, E.P. Training teachers and leaders to recognize and acknowledge creative behavior among disadvantaged children. *Gifted Child Quarterly*, 1972, *16*, 3–10.

Describes the "creative positives" of the disadvantaged gifted child and can assist in training teachers to recognize creative behavior.

Torrance, E.P., & Kaufman, F. Teacher education for career education of the gifted and talented. *Gifted Child Quarterly*, 1977, *21*, 176–185.

It is important to build a teacher education program that will provide teachers with the concepts, skills, and strategies to guide the gifted in career education. Specific learning activities (for teachers), which fuse the objectives of traditional subject matter, career education, and gifted and talented education, are included.

University of Georgia. *Graduate Study in Educational Psychology. (Bulletin of the Department of Educational Psychology).* Athens: College of Education, 1977–78.

>   *Contains the objectives, requirements, and course of study for the degree in gifted and talented at this university.*

Walker, J.J. Gifted teacher, know thyself. Gifted Child Quarterly, 1973, *17,* 288–292.

>   Several instruments are compared which introduce teachers to and familiarize them with (1) the concept of self-assessment and (2) the ten categories of the Flanders Verbal Interaction Analysis System and its application to classroom situations.

Weigand, J. (Ed.). *Developing teacher competencies.* Englewood Cliffs, NJ: Prentice-Hall, 1972.

>   Gives step-by-step directions in establishing competencies to service school systems and their teachers.

TEACHER CHARACTERISTICS AND COMPETENCIES—ROLE OF THE TEACHER

Bachtold, M. The creative personality and the ideal pupil revisited. *Journal of Creative Behavior,* 1974, *8,* 47–54.

>   Bachtold replicates the findings of earlier researchers, which demonstrate that teachers do not reinforce behaviors deemed creative in the classroom.

Barbe, W.B., & Frierson, E.C. Teaching the gifted: A new frame of reference. In W.B. Barbe & J.S. Renzulli (Eds.), *Psychology and education of the gifted.* New York: Halstead Press, 1975.

>   The teacher can be a learner-participant in a process-oriented classroom.

Bishop E. Successful teachers of the gifted. *Exceptional Children,* 1968, *34,* 317–325.

>   Bishop studied "personal and social traits and behaviors, professional attitudes and educational viewpoints, and classroom behavior patterns of effective teachers of gifted high school students." This article has implications for recruitment, selection, and training of teachers.

Coletta, A.J. Reflective and didactic styles for teachers of young gifted and poor children. *Gifted Child Quarterly,* 1975, *19,* 230–240.

>   A discussion of strategies teachers might use in implementing teaching styles.

Foster, F.P. The hu9man relationships of creative individuals. *Journal of Creative Behavior,* 1968, *2,* 111–118.

>   A review of literature that examines the relationships creative individuals have with others.

Frasier, M.M. The third dimension. *Gifted Child Quarterly,* 1977, *21,* 207–212.

>   Focuses on the preparation of teachers for their roles as "change agents" and public relations advocates.

Gold, M. *Education of the intellectually gifted.* Columbus, OH: Merrill, 1965.

>   Chapter 17, "Teachers for gifted children," is a good review of knowledge about skills, teacher characteristics, and preparation patterns as they existed in the early 60s. A preference is indicated for in-service education.

Gowan, J. & Torrance, P., (Eds.). *Educating the ablest*. Itasca, IL: F.E. Peacock, 1971.

A book of readings by major authors about the education of gifted children.

Guilford, J.P. *The nature of human intelligence*. New York: McGraw-Hill, 1967.

Guilford sets forth his Structure of Intellect Theory. Man is capable of at least 120 different intellectual abilities. Each one is a combination of an intellectual *operation*, some kind of informational *content* and a *product* or structuring of that content.

Guilford, J.P. *The analysis of intelligence*. New York: McGraw-Hill, 1971.

Guilford, J.P. *Way beyond the IQ*. Buffalo, NY: Creative Education Foundation, 1977.

Methods of testing and developing those intellectual abilities not ordinarily tapped in the classroom.

Hollingworth, L. *Children above 180 IQ*. New York: Harcourt, Brace, and World, 1942.

The behavioral problems of gifted children are discussed in relationship to degree of intelligence.

Kaplan, S. *Providing programs for the gifted and talented: A handbook*. Ventura, CA: Office of the Ventura County Superintendent of Schools, 1974.

This very complete handbook should be read by anyone initiating or expanding a program for the gifted. It contains a section on curriculum development, with discussions of practice worksheets for various instructional models. The final section deals with in-service training.

Krathwohl, D., Bloom, B., & Masia, B. *Taxonomy of educational objectives: Affective domain*. New York: McKay, 1964.

Presents a hierarchy of stage components in the affective domain developed by Bloom and his associates. Descriptions and behaviors are cited that exemplify each stage of development.

Malone, E.C., & Moonan, W.J. Behavioral identification of gifted children. *Gifted Child Quarterly*, 1975, *19*, 301–306.

The behavioral characteristics of gifted individuals are presented as being so distinctive as to separate them from the general population.

Meeker, M.N. *The structure of intellect: Its interpretation and uses*. Columbus, OH: Merrill, 1969.

Meeker develops practical applications of Guilford's theory. Sections include an assessment of IQ tests according to the SOI and suggested activities within curriculum areas to develop various skills.

North Carolina State Department of Public Instruction. *Competency-based program for certification—Gifted and talented*. Raleigh: 1976.

This includes (1) an explanation of the North Carolina competency based criteria for certification and (2) several appendices considering such topics as teaching strategies, sample instructional plans, and a bibliography for prospective teachers.

Osborn, A.R. *Applied imagination*. New York: Scribner, 1953.

According to the author, creativity is a teachable art. This book tells how to develop creative potential and to use that creativity to better our personal and occupational lives.

Parnes, J., Noller, R.B., & Biondi, A.M. *Guide to creative action.* New York: Scribner, 1977.

> A reference book, along with learning and instructional guides to help the teacher understand and deliberately develop creative behavior. It includes significant articles, and practical exercises, as well as a bibliography of films, tests, and books dealing with creativity.

Phenix, H. *Realms of meaning.* New York: McGraw-Hill, 1964.

> An inquiry into the various disciplines that asks, "What do you know when you say 'I know' in each of those areas." The examination of philosophy and methodology within and between the disciplines offers a unique resource for those teachers wishing to create a "laboratory environment" where all fields of knowledge are interrelated.

Renz, P., & Christoplos, F. Toward an operational definition of giftedness. *Journal of Creative Behavior,* 1968, 2, 91–96.

> An operational definition of giftedness is presented, which is based on a child's ability to develop though three steps of interactions between himself and the environment.

Renzulli, J.S. *New directions in creativity.* Evanston, IL: Harper & Row, 1973.

Renzulli, J.S. *The enrichment triad model: A guide for developing defensible programs for the gifted and talented.* Wethersfield, CT: Creative Learning Press, 1977.

> The triad model describes a type of programming for gifted children appropriate from the upper elementary grades on up. General exploratory experiences and group training in creativity lead to student participation in problem-solving and real-life investigations in areas of his or her own interest.

Saino, J., & Turner, J.R. *Why doesn't an igloo melt inside? A handbook for teachers of the academically gifted and talented* (Rev. ed.). Tennessee: Memphis City School System, 1978.

> Some of the more useful parts are sections on group discussions and effective questioning techniques, with emphasis on the proper use of questioning through sudy and application of Bloom's Taxonomy. There are also excellent sections on organizing mini-studies and independent projects.

Sanders, M. *Classroom questions: What kinds?* New York: Harper & Row, 1966.

> Bloom's taxonomy applied to the art of classroom questioning. Sanders is very specific: he goes through every level of the taxonomy with rationale for and how-to in question and development at each level.

Taba, H., Levine, S., & Elzey, F.F. *Thinking in elementary school children.* (USOE Cooperative Research Project #1574). San Francisco: San Francisco State College, 1964.

> Taba created a social studies curriculum based on developmental learning theory and designed to "lift" children's thinking from the lower to the higher cognitive levels. Her research showed that teachers trained in the use of this curriculum could indeed move children's thinking from concrete to formal more rapidly than would be expected strictly by maturation.

Torrance, P.E. Psychology of gifted children and youth. In W. Cruickshank (Ed.), *Psychology of gifted children and youth.* Englewood Cliffs, NJ: Prentice-Hall, 1971. Pp. 557–558.

> The problems of attaining a stable and positive self-concept for the gifted child are discussed with suggested strategies for school personnel.

Torrance, P.E., & Myers, R.E. *Creative learning and teaching.* New York: Dodd, Mead, 1973.

A very general book on setting up and maintaining a classroom atmosphere which encourages creativity and creative thinking and avoids the fourth grade "creativity slump."

Williams, F.E. Training children to be creative may have little effect on original classroom performance. *California Journal on Educational Research,* 1966, *17,* 73–79.

Research seems to indicate that the production of original responses (often used as a measure of creative ability) is highly related to the amount of knowledge possessed by a student. This seems to call for teaching strategies that guide the development of cognitive skills in such a way as to sharpen the ability to make new associations.

Williams, F.E. Models for encouraging creativity in the classroom by integrating cognitive-affective behaviors. *Educational Technology,* 1969, *9,* 7–13.

Williams presents a morphological approach based to some extent on the Guilford model and designed to implement certain thinking and feeling processes that are related to creativity in the classroom. There are 864 possible combinations of teaching strategies, subject matter areas, and cognitive and affective behaviors.

SKILLS AND KNOWLEDGE

Bloom, B.S. *Taxonomy of educational objectives: The classification of educational goals, Handbook I: Cognitive domain.* New York: McKay, 1956.

The goals of the educational process are presented as a hierarchy of intellectual skills, each new goal assuming mastery of the ones below. The intellectual processes of analysis, synthesis, and evaluation are considered the higher level cognitive processes. This book can provide background on developing curriculum to force the use of these higher level processes.

de Bono, E. *Lateral thinking: Creativity step by step.* New York: Harper & Row, 1970.

Creativity can be developed, according to de Bono, by the insightful rearrangement of available information.

Bruner, J.S. *Toward a theory of instruction.* Cambridge, MA: Harvard University Press, 1966.

This series of essays sets forth some of Bruner's ideas on the various means of assisting children's growth and development.

Dunn, R., & Dunn, K. *Practical approaches to individualizing instruction.* West Nyack, NY: Parker, 1972.

A guide for teachers, at all levels, in the use of contracts, learning activity packages, interest centers, and simulations which can individualize student instruction and allow in-depth work in any field of knowledge or interest.

Gallagher, J.J. *Teaching the gifted child.* Boston: Allyn & Bacon, 1975.

Strategies, programs, and research presented as they affect the instruction of the gifted. Both the cognitive and affective needs are discussed.

Gray, C.E., & Youngs, R.C. *Instructional strategies for creative hypothesizing: A training program. Final report.* Normal: Illinois State University, Teacher Education Project, 1971, (ERIC ED 054 040)

Gray, C.E., & Youngs, R.C. Utilizing the divergent production matrix of the structure of intellect model in the development of teaching strategies. *Gifted Child Quarterly*, 1975,
19, 290–300.

Describes a program in which teachers are trained "to facilitate creative problem-
solving on the part of their pupils."

Guilford, J.P. *Intelligence, creativity and their educational implications*. San Diego, CA:
Knapp, 1968.

Our classroom and testing procedures are almost entirely geared to memory and
convergent thinking. We have not begun to explore divergent thinking, which Guilford
feels is th foundation of creative behavior, or evaluation in the classroom.

Hughes, H.K. The enhancement of creativity. *Journal of Creative Behavior*, 1969, *2*, 73–83.

Based on knowledge of characteristics of creative, mature scientists. Activities are
suggested for enhancing creativity.

Nelson, J.B., & Cleland, D.J. The role of the teachers of gifted and creative children. In W.B.
Barbe & J.S. Renzulli *Psychology and education of the gifted*. New York: Halstead
Press, 1975.

Attitudes and behaviors that foster a climate that favors the development of creativity
and talent are detailed. The focus is on the orientation the teacher assumes in relationship to the student.

Neuman, E. A conversation with Jim Gallagher. In B.O. Boston (Ed.), *Gifted and talented:
Developing elementary and secondary school programs*. The Council for Exceptional
Children, Reston, VA: 1975, pp. 29–37.

Emphasis is on the training of "facilitators" in the education of the gifted at all levels,
people who understand and empathize with the system within which they work and
have the patience and perseverance to have maximum impact on change within that
system.

Stanley, J.D., Keating, D.P. & Fox, L.H. (Eds.). *Mathematical talent: Discovery, description,
and development*. Baltimore, MD: Johns Hopkins University Press, 1974.

This collection of scholarly articles deals with studies related to both cognitive and
affective aspects of adolescent precocity. Implications for the teacher are discussed in
relation to the findings.

Thompson, F.K. *Humane defined: A definition of self as humane teacher*. Unpublished doctoral dissertation, Teachers College, Columbia University, 1978.

Torrance, E.P. Can we teach children to think creatively? *Journal of Creative Behavior*, 1972,
6, 114–143.

Torrance discusses 142 studies of effectiveness in methods of teaching creativity.

Torrance, E.P. Readiness of teachers of gifted to learn from culturally different gifted children.
Gifted Child Quarterly, 1974, *18*, 137–145.

Torrance advocates having gifted disadvantaged children instruct their teachers in
some of the things they know well.

Torrance, E.P., & Torrance, P. Combining creative problem-solving with creative expression
activities. *Journal of Creative Behavior*, 1972, *6*, 1–10.

Techniques for working with creative disadvantaged children are described, and curriculum suggestions for teachers are offered.

Williams, F.E. Assessing pupil-teacher behaviors related to a cognitive-affective teaching model, *Journal of Research and Development in Education,* 1971, *4,* 14–22.

> Williams' model is discussed and strategies are presented to encourage creativity in the classroom.

GUIDANCE SKILLS FOR TEACHER TRAINERS

Brammer, L.M. *The helping relationships.* Englewood Cliffs, NJ: Prentice-Hall, 1973.

> The process and skills necessary for counseling and helping are detailed with insight and clarity. A good resource for both teacher educators and administrators.

Bunker, M.R. Beyond in-service: Toward staff renewal. *Journal of Teacher Education,* 1977, *28,* 31–34.

> An innovative approach to in-service staff renewal. Emphasis on a humanistic experiential approach to teacher training exemplified by the model's successful utilization in Amherst, Massachusetts.

Combs, A.W., Avila, D.L. & Purkey, W.W. *Helping relationships.* Boston: Allyn & Bacon, 1971.

> Strategies to assist the "helping professions" in providing more supportive and successful services to their clients. This is a particularly valuable resource for the supervisor of student teachers.

Combs, A.W., Avila, D.L., & Purkey, W.W. *The helping relationship sourcebook.* Boston: Allyn & Bacon, 1972.

> A compilation of articles that explore various aspects of the helping professions is presented as well as references for specific investigations into techniques and theory.

Gallagher, J.J. Personnel for high performance children. In J.J. Gallagher (Ed.), *Teaching the gifted child.* Boston: Allyn & Bacon, 1975. Pp. 282–283.

Goldhammer, R. *Clinical supervision.* New York: Rinehart and Winston, 1969.

> A detailed description of various methods for the supervision of teachers.

Gowan, J.C. & Bruch, C. What makes a creative person a creative teacher. In E.P. Torrance & J.C. Gowan (Eds.), *Educating the ablest.* New York: Peacock, 1971, pp. 165–170.

> A study of descriptors for teaching characteristics of teachers of the gifted.

Greenwood, G.E., Good, T.L., & Siegel, B.L. *Problem situations in teaching.* New York: Harper & Row, 1971.

> Twenty representative case studies with suggested strategies for attacking the teaching problem in the cases.

Greer, M., & Rubenstein, B. *Will the real teacher please stand up: A primer in humanistic education.* Pacific Palisades, CA: Goodyear, 1972.

> Methods and techniques for the classroom teacher are detailed that relate to the affective domain.

Meyers-Briggs inventory-type indicator-manual: Introduction to type. Princeton, NJ: Educational Testing Service, 1970.

> Different personality types of teachers are discussed in terms of their effects on gifted students.

Raths, L., Harmin, M., & Simon, S.G. *Values and teaching*. Columbus, OH: Merrill, 1966.

The notion of clarifying values in making decisions is examined. The foundations for values clarification are outlined with implications for both student and teacher.

Rogers, C.R. *Freedom to learn*. Columbus, OH: Merrill, 1969

Fundamental assumptions about the role of environment on the learning process of the individual are discussed with sensitivity and depth.

Simon, S.B. The teacher educator in value development. *Phi Delta Kappan,* 1972, *52,* 649–651.

The role of the teacher educator is examined in terms of values clarification in relation to the training of teachers.

Wilson, F.T. The motivation of the gifted and teacher education. *Journal of Teacher Education,* 1961, *12,* 179–184.

Wilson advocates strengthening pre-service teacher education programs to help teachers gain the abilities, the knowledge, and the materials necessary to recognize, accept, and motivate gifted children and to maximize their potential.

INDEX

Affective development, 11
Arithmetic, 4
Art, 4 (table 2), 6
Attention span, 10

Balance in teacher-training programs, 42–3
Bloom's taxonomy of the cognitive domain, 11, 21–2 (table 3)
Brainstorming, 21
Bruch, K, 3

Certification by states of teachers of the gifted, 2–6, 7
Characteristics of teachers of the gifted, 11–4; self understanding, 15–8; sensitivity, 16–8
Characteristics of the gifted, 9–11
Cleland, D.L., 10
Classrooms, 22
Cognitive processes, 5 (table 2); development of, 11–4, 43
College and university programs for teachers of the gifted and talented, 3–7
Combs, A.W., 15
Competency-based teacher education programs (CBTE), 41–5
Council for Exceptional Children, 29, 42
Creativity, 5 (table 2), 10–1; in teachers, 13–4
Curriculum, competency-based, 27–45
Curriculum design, 5 (table 2), 11; materials for, 6, 8; for teacher education, 32–45

Democratic education, 44
Decision making, 33 (fig. 5)
Divergent thinking, 11, 21 (table 3)

Education, study of, 27–45
Enrichment, 6
Ethical considerations, 22

Evaluation of teacher education programs, 29, 31–2 (fig. 4), 39, 41–5

Feedback on teaching programs, 28–9, 32–5, 42, 44
Films, 21 (table 3), 25
Funding, federal, for education of the gifted, 2, 11

Games, 6, 21 (table 3)
Gifted and talented, definition, 9–11
Gifted and Talented Education, Office of. See: United States Office of Education
Gold, Milton J., 13
Guilford's Structure of Intellect model, 11

Horace Mann-Lincoln Institute of School Experimentation, 1
Humor, 10
Hypothesizing, 24

Identification of giftedness, 9–11
Inferring, 24
In-service training of teachers, 6, 9, 28
Intellectual skills: hypothesizing, 24; inferring, 24
Internship of teachers, 5

Johns Hopkins University, 10

Knowledge required of teachers, 18–23: of content, 18–9; of teaching processes, 19–23 (table 3)
Krathwohl's taxonomy of the affective domain, 22–3

Language arts, 6
Las Vegas, NV, school system, 6
Learning difficulties, 5
Liberal education, 37–8